50 Middle Eastern Vegetarian Feast Recipes for Home

By: Kelly Johnson

Table of Contents

- Falafel with Tahini Sauce
- Baba Ganoush
- Hummus with Olive Oil and Paprika
- Tabouleh Salad
- Stuffed Grape Leaves (Dolma)
- Muhammara (Red Pepper and Walnut Dip)
- Fattoush Salad
- Lentil Soup with Lemon and Spinach
- Eggplant Moussaka
- Spinach Fatayer (Spinach Triangles)
- Vegetarian Kebabs with Grilled Vegetables
- Tabbouleh Stuffed Bell Peppers
- Za'atar Flatbread
- Labneh (Yogurt Cheese)
- Mujadara (Lentils and Rice with Caramelized Onions)
- Lebanese Fattoush Salad
- Turkish Imam Bayildi (Stuffed Eggplant)
- Moroccan Couscous with Roasted Vegetables
- Persian Sabzi Polo (Herb Rice)
- Stuffed Zucchini with Rice and Pine Nuts
- Turkish Bulgur Pilaf with Chickpeas and Tomatoes
- Egyptian Kushari (Rice, Lentils, and Pasta)
- Muhammara Stuffed Mushrooms
- Lebanese Mujadara with Cucumber Yogurt Salad
- Persian Kashk-e Bademjan (Eggplant Dip)
- Moroccan Chickpea Tagine with Apricots and Almonds
- Lebanese Foul Mudammas (Fava Beans)
- Turkish Red Lentil Soup (Mercimek Çorbası)
- Persian Borani Esfenaj (Spinach Yogurt Dip)
- Lebanese Batata Harra (Spicy Potatoes)
- Moroccan Vegetable Tagine with Couscous
- Turkish Börek with Spinach and Feta
- Persian Jeweled Rice (Javaher Polow)
- Stuffed Bell Peppers with Rice and Lentils
- Lebanese Tabbouleh Stuffed Avocados

- Turkish Imam Bayildi with Feta
- Moroccan Carrot Salad with Cumin Dressing
- Persian Adas Polo (Lentil Rice)
- Lebanese Mujadara with Mint Yogurt Sauce
- Turkish Stuffed Eggplant with Tomato Sauce
- Moroccan Zaalouk (Eggplant and Tomato Dip)
- Persian Kookoo Sabzi (Herb Frittata)
- Lebanese Spinach Pies (Fatayer Sabanekh)
- Turkish Mezze Platter with Olives, Cheese, and Bread
- Moroccan Lentil Salad with Roasted Vegetables
- Persian Eggplant Stew (Gheimeh Bademjan)
- Lebanese Lentil Salad with Feta and Mint
- Turkish Börek with Potato and Cheese
- Moroccan Vegetable Bastilla
- Persian Lentil and Spinach Soup (Ash-e Reshteh)

Falafel with Tahini Sauce

Ingredients:

For Falafel:

- 1 cup dried chickpeas
- 1 small onion, roughly chopped
- 3 cloves garlic
- 1/4 cup fresh parsley, chopped
- 1/4 cup fresh cilantro, chopped
- 1 teaspoon ground cumin
- 1 teaspoon ground coriander
- 1/4 teaspoon cayenne pepper (optional)
- Salt to taste
- 1 teaspoon baking powder
- 4 tablespoons all-purpose flour
- Vegetable oil for frying

For Tahini Sauce:

- 1/2 cup tahini paste
- 1/4 cup water
- 2 tablespoons lemon juice
- 2 cloves garlic, minced
- Salt to taste
- Chopped fresh parsley for garnish (optional)

Instructions:

Prepare Chickpeas:
- Place dried chickpeas in a large bowl and cover with water. Let soak overnight or for at least 8 hours. Drain well before using.

Make Falafel Mixture:
- In a food processor, combine soaked and drained chickpeas, onion, garlic, parsley, cilantro, cumin, coriander, cayenne pepper (if using), and salt. Pulse until mixture is finely chopped but not pureed.
- Transfer the mixture to a bowl and stir in baking powder and flour until well combined. The mixture should be thick enough to hold its shape when formed into balls.

Form Falafel Balls:
- With damp hands, shape the mixture into small balls, about 1 to 1 1/2 inches in diameter, and slightly flatten them into patties.

Fry Falafel:

- Heat vegetable oil in a deep skillet or pot over medium heat. Fry the falafel in batches until golden brown and crispy, about 3-4 minutes per side. Use a slotted spoon to transfer cooked falafel to a paper towel-lined plate to drain excess oil.

Prepare Tahini Sauce:
- In a small bowl, whisk together tahini paste, water, lemon juice, minced garlic, and salt until smooth and creamy. Adjust consistency with more water if needed.

Serve:
- Serve falafel warm with tahini sauce drizzled over the top. Garnish with chopped fresh parsley if desired.

Enjoy your homemade Falafel with Tahini Sauce!

Feel free to adjust the seasoning or ingredients according to your taste preferences. If you have any allergies or dietary restrictions, please let me know, and I can suggest alternative ingredients.

Baba Ganoush

Ingredients:

- 2 medium-sized eggplants
- 2 cloves of garlic, minced
- 1/4 cup tahini
- Juice of 1 lemon
- 2 tablespoons olive oil, plus extra for drizzling
- Salt, to taste
- Chopped parsley, for garnish (optional)
- Pita bread, crackers, or vegetables, for serving

Instructions:

Preheat your oven to 400°F (200°C).
Wash the eggplants and prick them several times with a fork to prevent them from bursting while roasting.
Place the whole eggplants on a baking sheet lined with parchment paper or aluminum foil.
Roast the eggplants in the preheated oven for about 45-50 minutes, or until they are completely soft and collapsed.
Remove the eggplants from the oven and let them cool slightly.
Once cooled, slice the eggplants in half lengthwise and scoop out the flesh into a colander set over a bowl. Let the eggplant flesh drain for about 15-20 minutes to remove excess moisture.
Transfer the drained eggplant flesh to a food processor or blender. Add the minced garlic, tahini, lemon juice, olive oil, and salt to taste.
Blend the mixture until smooth and creamy. If the mixture is too thick, you can add a little bit of water or more olive oil to reach your desired consistency.
Taste and adjust the seasoning, adding more salt or lemon juice if needed.
Transfer the baba ganoush to a serving bowl. Drizzle with extra olive oil and garnish with chopped parsley, if desired.
Serve the baba ganoush with pita bread, crackers, or fresh vegetables for dipping.

Enjoy your homemade baba ganoush straight from the cookbook!

Hummus with Olive Oil and Paprika

Ingredients:

- 1 can (15 ounces) chickpeas (garbanzo beans), drained and rinsed
- 2 cloves garlic, minced
- 3 tablespoons tahini
- Juice of 1 lemon
- 2 tablespoons olive oil, plus extra for drizzling
- 1/2 teaspoon ground cumin
- Salt, to taste
- Water, as needed
- Paprika, for garnish
- Chopped parsley or cilantro, for garnish (optional)

Instructions:

In a food processor, combine the drained chickpeas, minced garlic, tahini, lemon juice, olive oil, ground cumin, and a pinch of salt.
Process the mixture until smooth. If the hummus is too thick, you can add a tablespoon or two of water while processing until you reach your desired consistency.
Taste the hummus and adjust the seasoning, adding more salt or lemon juice if needed.
Once the hummus is smooth and seasoned to your liking, transfer it to a serving bowl.
Drizzle extra olive oil over the top of the hummus and sprinkle with paprika for a colorful garnish.
If desired, sprinkle chopped parsley or cilantro over the hummus for added freshness and flavor.
Serve the hummus with pita bread, crackers, or fresh vegetables for dipping.
Enjoy your homemade hummus with olive oil and paprika as a delicious appetizer or snack!

Tabouleh Salad

Ingredients:

- 1 cup bulgur wheat
- 2 cups finely chopped fresh parsley
- 1 cup finely chopped fresh mint leaves
- 2 medium tomatoes, diced
- 1/2 cup finely chopped green onions or scallions
- 1/4 cup lemon juice (about 2-3 lemons)
- 1/4 cup extra virgin olive oil
- Salt, to taste
- Black pepper, to taste
- Optional: 1/2 cup diced cucumber, 1/4 cup diced red onion, 1/4 cup chopped fresh cilantro

Instructions:

Rinse the bulgur wheat in a fine-mesh sieve under cold water. Drain well and transfer to a large mixing bowl.
Pour boiling water over the bulgur wheat, ensuring it's completely submerged. Let it sit for about 20-30 minutes, or until the bulgur is tender and has absorbed the water.
Fluff the bulgur with a fork and let it cool to room temperature.
Once cooled, add the chopped parsley, mint, tomatoes, green onions, and any optional ingredients (such as cucumber, red onion, or cilantro) to the bowl with the bulgur wheat.
In a small bowl, whisk together the lemon juice, olive oil, salt, and black pepper to make the dressing.
Pour the dressing over the salad and toss well to combine, ensuring all the ingredients are evenly coated.
Taste the salad and adjust the seasoning if necessary, adding more salt, pepper, or lemon juice according to your preference.
Cover the tabbouleh salad and refrigerate for at least 1 hour to allow the flavors to meld.
Before serving, give the salad a final toss and adjust the seasoning if needed. You can also drizzle a little extra olive oil over the top for added richness.
Serve chilled or at room temperature as a side dish or appetizer.

Enjoy your homemade tabbouleh salad, bursting with fresh flavors and vibrant colors!

Stuffed Grape Leaves (Dolma)

Ingredients:

- 1 jar (about 8 ounces) grape leaves in brine, rinsed and drained
- 1 cup short-grain rice (such as Arborio or sushi rice)
- 1 large onion, finely chopped
- 2 tablespoons olive oil
- 1/4 cup pine nuts or chopped walnuts (optional)
- 1/4 cup currants or chopped dried apricots (optional)
- 2 tablespoons chopped fresh dill
- 2 tablespoons chopped fresh mint
- 2 tablespoons chopped fresh parsley
- Juice of 1 lemon
- Salt, to taste
- Black pepper, to taste
- 1 1/2 cups vegetable broth or water
- Greek yogurt or tzatziki sauce, for serving (optional)

Instructions:

Prepare the grape leaves: If using grape leaves from a jar, rinse them thoroughly under cold water to remove excess salt. Gently separate the leaves and set aside.

In a large skillet, heat the olive oil over medium heat. Add the chopped onion and sauté until softened and translucent, about 5 minutes.

Add the rice to the skillet and cook, stirring constantly, for 2-3 minutes to toast the rice slightly.

Stir in the pine nuts or chopped walnuts (if using) and currants or chopped dried apricots (if using), along with the chopped dill, mint, and parsley. Cook for another 1-2 minutes to toast the nuts and incorporate the flavors.

Remove the skillet from the heat and stir in the lemon juice. Season the mixture with salt and black pepper to taste.

To assemble the stuffed grape leaves, place a grape leaf shiny side down on a clean work surface. Trim off any tough stems.

Place about 1 tablespoon of the rice filling near the stem end of the grape leaf.

Fold the bottom of the leaf over the filling, then fold in the sides, and roll up tightly into a compact cylinder.

Repeat with the remaining grape leaves and filling mixture.

Arrange the stuffed grape leaves snugly in a single layer in a large pot or deep skillet. Pack them tightly to prevent them from unraveling during cooking.

Pour the vegetable broth or water over the stuffed grape leaves, ensuring they are just covered with liquid.

Place a heatproof plate or lid directly on top of the stuffed grape leaves to weigh them down and prevent them from floating during cooking.

Cover the pot or skillet and bring the liquid to a simmer over medium-low heat. Cook the stuffed grape leaves for 30-40 minutes, or until the rice is tender and the grape leaves are softened.

Once cooked, remove the stuffed grape leaves from the heat and let them cool slightly in the pot before serving.

Serve the stuffed grape leaves warm or at room temperature, optionally accompanied by Greek yogurt or tzatziki sauce for dipping.

Enjoy your homemade stuffed grape leaves (dolma) as a flavorful appetizer or side dish!

Stuffed Grape Leaves (Dolma)

Ingredients:

- 1 jar (about 8 ounces) grape leaves in brine, rinsed and drained
- 1 cup long-grain rice
- 1 medium onion, finely chopped
- 1/4 cup pine nuts, toasted
- 1/4 cup currants or raisins
- 1/4 cup chopped fresh parsley
- 1/4 cup chopped fresh dill
- 1/4 cup chopped fresh mint
- Juice of 2 lemons
- 1/4 cup extra virgin olive oil
- Salt and pepper, to taste
- Water, as needed
- Greek yogurt, for serving (optional)

Instructions:

In a large bowl, combine the rice, chopped onion, toasted pine nuts, currants or raisins, chopped parsley, dill, mint, lemon juice, olive oil, salt, and pepper. Mix well to combine.
Place a grape leaf on a clean work surface, shiny side down and stem side facing you.
Place about 1 tablespoon of the rice mixture near the stem end of the grape leaf.
Fold the bottom of the leaf over the filling, then fold in the sides, and roll up tightly into a cigar shape.
Repeat with the remaining grape leaves and filling mixture.
Line the bottom of a large pot with any torn or unused grape leaves.
Arrange the stuffed grape leaves, seam side down, in the pot in tight layers.
Once all the stuffed grape leaves are arranged in the pot, place a heavy plate on top to keep them from unraveling during cooking.
Pour enough water into the pot to cover the stuffed grape leaves.
Cover the pot and bring the water to a boil over medium heat. Once boiling, reduce the heat to low and simmer for about 45-50 minutes, or until the rice is fully cooked and tender.
Once cooked, remove the stuffed grape leaves from the pot and let them cool slightly before serving.
Serve the stuffed grape leaves warm or at room temperature, optionally accompanied by Greek yogurt for dipping.

Enjoy your homemade stuffed grape leaves (dolma)! They make a delicious appetizer or side dish.

Muhammara (Red Pepper and Walnut Dip)

Ingredients:

- 3 large red bell peppers
- 1 cup walnuts
- 1/2 cup breadcrumbs
- 3 cloves garlic, minced
- 2 tablespoons lemon juice
- 2 tablespoons pomegranate molasses
- 1 teaspoon ground cumin
- 1 teaspoon paprika
- 1/2 teaspoon cayenne pepper (optional, for extra heat)
- 1/4 teaspoon salt, or to taste
- 1/4 cup extra virgin olive oil, plus extra for drizzling
- Chopped fresh parsley or mint, for garnish (optional)
- Pomegranate seeds, for garnish (optional)

Instructions:

Preheat your oven to 400°F (200°C). Place the whole red bell peppers on a baking sheet lined with parchment paper or aluminum foil.

Roast the red peppers in the preheated oven for about 30-40 minutes, or until they are charred and blistered on the outside, turning them occasionally to ensure even roasting.

Remove the roasted red peppers from the oven and transfer them to a heatproof bowl. Cover the bowl with plastic wrap or aluminum foil and let the peppers steam for about 10-15 minutes. This will make it easier to peel off the skins.

Once the peppers have steamed, carefully peel off the skins and remove the seeds and membranes. Discard the skins and seeds, and chop the roasted peppers into smaller pieces.

In a food processor, combine the roasted red peppers, walnuts, breadcrumbs, minced garlic, lemon juice, pomegranate molasses, ground cumin, paprika, cayenne pepper (if using), and salt.

Pulse the mixture until it becomes a coarse paste. Scrape down the sides of the food processor bowl as needed to ensure all ingredients are well incorporated.

With the food processor running, gradually drizzle in the olive oil until the mixture becomes smooth and creamy. You may need to add a bit more olive oil if the dip is too thick.

Taste the muhammara and adjust the seasoning, adding more salt, lemon juice, or spices if needed to suit your taste.

Transfer the muhammara to a serving bowl. Drizzle with a little extra olive oil and garnish with chopped fresh parsley or mint and pomegranate seeds, if desired.

Serve the muhammara with pita bread, crackers, or fresh vegetables for dipping.

Enjoy your homemade muhammara as a delicious and vibrant dip or spread!

Fattoush Salad

Ingredients:

For the salad:

- 4 cups mixed salad greens (such as romaine lettuce, arugula, and/or watercress), torn into bite-sized pieces
- 1 cucumber, diced
- 2 tomatoes, diced
- 1 bell pepper (red or green), diced
- 1 small red onion, thinly sliced
- 1/4 cup chopped fresh parsley
- 1/4 cup chopped fresh mint
- 1/4 cup chopped green onions (optional)
- 1/2 cup sliced radishes (optional)
- 1/2 cup chopped fresh cilantro (optional)

For the toasted pita:

- 2 large pita bread rounds
- 2 tablespoons olive oil
- 1/2 teaspoon sumac (optional)
- Salt, to taste

For the dressing:

- 1/4 cup extra virgin olive oil
- 2 tablespoons lemon juice
- 1 tablespoon red wine vinegar
- 1 clove garlic, minced
- 1 teaspoon ground sumac (optional)
- 1/2 teaspoon ground cumin
- Salt, to taste
- Black pepper, to taste

Instructions:

Preheat your oven to 375°F (190°C).
Cut the pita bread into bite-sized pieces and place them on a baking sheet. Drizzle with olive oil, sprinkle with sumac (if using), and season with salt. Toss to coat evenly.

Bake the pita bread in the preheated oven for 10-12 minutes, or until golden brown and crispy. Remove from the oven and let cool.
In a large salad bowl, combine the mixed salad greens, diced cucumber, diced tomatoes, diced bell pepper, sliced red onion, chopped parsley, chopped mint, and any optional ingredients such as green onions, radishes, or cilantro.
In a small bowl, whisk together the extra virgin olive oil, lemon juice, red wine vinegar, minced garlic, ground sumac (if using), ground cumin, salt, and black pepper to make the dressing.
Pour the dressing over the salad and toss well to coat all the ingredients evenly.
Just before serving, add the toasted pita bread to the salad and toss gently to combine.
Taste the salad and adjust the seasoning if necessary, adding more salt, lemon juice, or spices according to your preference.
Serve the fattoush salad immediately as a refreshing appetizer or side dish.

Enjoy your homemade fattoush salad with its vibrant flavors and textures!

Lentil Soup with Lemon and Spinach

Ingredients:

- 1 cup dried lentils (brown or green), rinsed and drained
- 1 onion, finely chopped
- 2 cloves garlic, minced
- 2 carrots, diced
- 2 stalks celery, diced
- 6 cups vegetable broth or water
- 1 teaspoon ground cumin
- 1 teaspoon ground coriander
- 1/2 teaspoon smoked paprika
- 1 bay leaf
- Salt and black pepper, to taste
- Zest and juice of 1 lemon
- 4 cups fresh spinach leaves, chopped
- 2 tablespoons olive oil
- Fresh parsley, chopped, for garnish (optional)

Instructions:

In a large pot, heat the olive oil over medium heat. Add the chopped onion and cook until softened and translucent, about 5 minutes. Add the minced garlic and cook for another minute, stirring frequently.

Add the diced carrots and celery to the pot, and cook for another 5 minutes, or until the vegetables start to soften.

Stir in the rinsed lentils, ground cumin, ground coriander, smoked paprika, bay leaf, salt, and black pepper. Cook for 1-2 minutes, stirring constantly to toast the spices.

Pour in the vegetable broth or water, and bring the soup to a boil. Reduce the heat to low, cover the pot, and simmer for about 20-25 minutes, or until the lentils are tender.

Once the lentils are cooked, remove the bay leaf from the soup. Using an immersion blender, blend the soup partially to achieve your desired consistency. You can leave some lentils whole for texture.

Stir in the chopped spinach leaves and let them wilt in the hot soup for a couple of minutes.

Add the lemon zest and juice to the soup, adjusting the amount to your taste preference. Stir well to incorporate.
Taste the soup and adjust the seasoning with salt and black pepper if needed.
Ladle the lentil soup into bowls and garnish with chopped fresh parsley, if desired.
Serve hot, optionally with a slice of crusty bread or a sprinkle of grated Parmesan cheese on top.

Enjoy your comforting and flavorful lentil soup with lemon and spinach!

Eggplant Moussaka

Ingredients:

For the eggplant layers:

- 2 large eggplants, sliced lengthwise into 1/4-inch thick slices
- Salt, for sprinkling
- Olive oil, for brushing

For the meat sauce:

- 1 lb (450g) ground lamb or beef
- 1 onion, finely chopped
- 2 cloves garlic, minced
- 1 can (14 oz/400g) diced tomatoes
- 2 tablespoons tomato paste
- 1 teaspoon dried oregano
- 1 teaspoon dried thyme
- 1 teaspoon ground cinnamon
- Salt and black pepper, to taste

For the béchamel sauce:

- 4 tablespoons unsalted butter
- 1/4 cup all-purpose flour
- 2 cups whole milk
- Pinch of nutmeg
- Salt and black pepper, to taste
- 1/2 cup grated Parmesan cheese

Instructions:

Preheat your oven to 400°F (200°C). Line a baking sheet with parchment paper. Place the eggplant slices on the prepared baking sheet. Sprinkle them with salt and let them sit for about 15-20 minutes to release excess moisture.
After 15-20 minutes, pat the eggplant slices dry with paper towels to remove the moisture. Brush both sides of the eggplant slices with olive oil.

Place the baking sheet in the preheated oven and bake the eggplant slices for about 15-20 minutes, or until they are softened and lightly browned. Remove from the oven and set aside.

While the eggplant is baking, prepare the meat sauce. In a large skillet or frying pan, heat a tablespoon of olive oil over medium heat. Add the chopped onion and minced garlic, and sauté until softened and fragrant.

Add the ground lamb or beef to the skillet and cook, breaking it up with a spoon, until browned and cooked through.

Stir in the diced tomatoes, tomato paste, dried oregano, dried thyme, ground cinnamon, salt, and black pepper. Simmer the sauce for about 10-15 minutes, allowing the flavors to meld. Remove from heat and set aside.

To make the béchamel sauce, melt the butter in a saucepan over medium heat. Once melted, whisk in the flour and cook for 1-2 minutes, stirring constantly, until the mixture is smooth and bubbly.

Gradually whisk in the milk, a little at a time, until the mixture is smooth and thickened. Stir in a pinch of nutmeg and season with salt and black pepper to taste.

Cook the béchamel sauce for a few more minutes, stirring constantly, until it thickens further.

Remove the saucepan from the heat and stir in the grated Parmesan cheese until melted and smooth.

To assemble the moussaka, grease a baking dish with olive oil. Arrange a layer of the baked eggplant slices on the bottom of the dish.

Spread half of the meat sauce over the eggplant layer.

Add another layer of eggplant slices on top of the meat sauce.

Spread the remaining meat sauce over the eggplant layer.

Pour the béchamel sauce over the top of the meat sauce layer, spreading it out evenly with a spatula.

Place the moussaka in the preheated oven and bake for about 40-45 minutes, or until the top is golden brown and bubbling.

Remove the moussaka from the oven and let it cool for a few minutes before slicing and serving.

Serve the eggplant moussaka warm, optionally garnished with chopped fresh parsley.

Enjoy your delicious homemade eggplant moussaka!

Spinach Fatayer (Spinach Triangles)

Ingredients:

For the dough:

- 2 cups all-purpose flour
- 1 teaspoon active dry yeast
- 1 teaspoon sugar
- 1/2 teaspoon salt
- 1/4 cup olive oil
- 3/4 cup warm water

For the spinach filling:

- 1 tablespoon olive oil
- 1 small onion, finely chopped
- 2 cloves garlic, minced
- 10 ounces (about 300g) fresh spinach, chopped
- 1/4 cup pine nuts, toasted
- 1 teaspoon ground sumac
- 1/2 teaspoon ground cumin
- Salt and black pepper, to taste

Instructions:

In a small bowl, dissolve the active dry yeast and sugar in warm water. Let it sit for about 5-10 minutes, or until foamy.

In a large mixing bowl, combine the flour and salt. Make a well in the center and pour in the yeast mixture and olive oil.

Stir the ingredients together until a dough forms. Turn the dough out onto a lightly floured surface and knead it for about 5-7 minutes, or until smooth and elastic. Add more flour if the dough is too sticky.

Place the dough in a lightly oiled bowl, cover with a clean kitchen towel or plastic wrap, and let it rise in a warm place for about 1-2 hours, or until doubled in size.

While the dough is rising, prepare the spinach filling. In a skillet, heat the olive oil over medium heat. Add the chopped onion and minced garlic, and sauté until softened and fragrant.

Add the chopped spinach to the skillet and cook, stirring frequently, until wilted and any excess moisture has evaporated.

Stir in the toasted pine nuts, ground sumac, ground cumin, salt, and black pepper. Cook for another 1-2 minutes, then remove the skillet from the heat and let the filling cool slightly.

Preheat your oven to 375°F (190°C). Line a baking sheet with parchment paper.

Once the dough has doubled in size, punch it down and divide it into equal-sized portions, about the size of a golf ball.

Roll out each portion of dough into a circle, about 1/8 inch thick.

Place a spoonful of the spinach filling in the center of each dough circle.

Fold the edges of the dough over the filling to form a triangle shape, pinching the edges tightly to seal.

Place the spinach fatayer on the prepared baking sheet, leaving some space between each one.

Bake the fatayer in the preheated oven for about 15-20 minutes, or until golden brown and cooked through.

Remove the fatayer from the oven and let them cool slightly before serving.

Serve the spinach fatayer warm or at room temperature as a delicious appetizer or snack.

Enjoy your homemade spinach fatayer!

Vegetarian Kebabs with Grilled Vegetables

Ingredients:

For the kebabs:

- 1 block extra firm tofu, pressed and cubed
- 1 red bell pepper, cut into chunks
- 1 yellow bell pepper, cut into chunks
- 1 zucchini, sliced into rounds
- 1 red onion, cut into chunks
- 8-10 cherry tomatoes
- 8-10 button mushrooms
- Wooden skewers, soaked in water for at least 30 minutes

For the marinade:

- 1/4 cup olive oil
- 2 tablespoons soy sauce or tamari
- 2 cloves garlic, minced
- 1 teaspoon smoked paprika
- 1 teaspoon ground cumin
- 1/2 teaspoon ground coriander
- 1/2 teaspoon ground black pepper
- Salt, to taste
- Juice of 1 lemon

Instructions:

In a mixing bowl, combine all the ingredients for the marinade and whisk until well combined.

Place the cubed tofu in a shallow dish or resealable plastic bag. Pour the marinade over the tofu and toss to coat evenly. Cover the dish or seal the bag and let the tofu marinate in the refrigerator for at least 30 minutes, or up to 2 hours, to allow the flavors to develop.

While the tofu is marinating, prepare the vegetables. Thread the marinated tofu cubes and prepared vegetables onto the soaked wooden skewers, alternating the ingredients as desired.

Preheat your grill to medium-high heat. If using a charcoal grill, wait until the coals are hot and glowing.

Lightly oil the grill grates to prevent the kebabs from sticking. Place the assembled kebabs on the grill and cook for about 8-10 minutes, turning occasionally, or until the vegetables are tender and lightly charred.
While the kebabs are grilling, you can brush them with any remaining marinade to keep them moist and flavorful.
Once the kebabs are cooked through and the vegetables are tender, remove them from the grill and transfer to a serving platter.
Serve the vegetarian kebabs with grilled vegetables hot off the grill, optionally garnished with chopped fresh herbs like parsley or cilantro.
Enjoy your delicious vegetarian kebabs with grilled vegetables as a main course or as part of a barbecue feast!

Feel free to customize the vegetables according to your preference, and you can also serve the kebabs with your favorite dipping sauce or tzatziki for extra flavor.

Tabbouleh Stuffed Bell Peppers

Ingredients:

- 4 large bell peppers (any color), halved and seeds removed
- 1 cup bulgur wheat
- 1 1/2 cups water
- 1/4 cup lemon juice
- 1/4 cup extra virgin olive oil
- 2 cups chopped fresh parsley
- 1 cup chopped fresh mint
- 2 tomatoes, diced
- 1 cucumber, diced
- 1/2 red onion, finely chopped
- Salt and black pepper, to taste
- Optional: crumbled feta cheese, for garnish

Instructions:

Preheat your oven to 375°F (190°C). Grease a baking dish with olive oil or cooking spray.
In a small saucepan, bring the water to a boil. Stir in the bulgur wheat, cover, and remove from heat. Let the bulgur wheat sit for about 15-20 minutes, or until it absorbs all the water and becomes tender. Fluff the bulgur with a fork and let it cool to room temperature.
In a large mixing bowl, combine the cooked bulgur wheat, chopped parsley, chopped mint, diced tomatoes, diced cucumber, and finely chopped red onion.
In a small bowl, whisk together the lemon juice, extra virgin olive oil, salt, and black pepper to make the dressing.
Pour the dressing over the tabbouleh mixture and toss to combine, ensuring all ingredients are evenly coated.
Place the halved bell peppers in the prepared baking dish, cut side up.
Spoon the tabbouleh mixture into each bell pepper half, pressing down gently to pack the filling.
Cover the baking dish with aluminum foil and bake the stuffed bell peppers in the preheated oven for about 30-35 minutes, or until the peppers are tender.
Remove the foil and continue baking for an additional 5-10 minutes, or until the tops are lightly golden.
Optional: If desired, sprinkle crumbled feta cheese over the stuffed bell peppers during the last 5 minutes of baking.
Remove the stuffed bell peppers from the oven and let them cool slightly before serving.
Serve the tabbouleh stuffed bell peppers warm as a flavorful and nutritious main dish or side dish.

Enjoy your delicious homemade tabbouleh stuffed bell peppers! They're packed with fresh flavors and make a wonderful addition to any meal.

Za'atar Flatbread

Ingredients:

For the dough:

- 2 cups all-purpose flour
- 1 teaspoon instant yeast
- 1 teaspoon sugar
- 1 teaspoon salt
- 2 tablespoons olive oil
- 3/4 cup warm water

For the topping:

- 2-3 tablespoons za'atar spice blend
- 2 tablespoons olive oil

Instructions:

In a large mixing bowl, combine the all-purpose flour, instant yeast, sugar, and salt.
Make a well in the center of the dry ingredients and pour in the olive oil and warm water.
Stir the ingredients together until a dough forms. Turn the dough out onto a lightly floured surface and knead it for about 5-7 minutes, or until smooth and elastic.
Place the dough in a lightly oiled bowl, cover with a clean kitchen towel or plastic wrap, and let it rise in a warm place for about 1 hour, or until doubled in size.
Preheat your oven to 425°F (220°C). Place a pizza stone or baking sheet in the oven to preheat.
Once the dough has doubled in size, punch it down and divide it into equal-sized portions, depending on how many flatbreads you want to make.
Roll out each portion of dough into a thin circle or oval shape, about 1/4 inch thick.
Place the rolled-out dough on a piece of parchment paper or a lightly floured surface.
In a small bowl, mix together the za'atar spice blend and olive oil to form a paste.
Spread a thin layer of the za'atar paste evenly over the surface of each flatbread.

Transfer the flatbreads, along with the parchment paper, onto the preheated pizza stone or baking sheet in the oven.
Bake the flatbreads for about 10-12 minutes, or until golden brown and crisp around the edges.
Remove the flatbreads from the oven and let them cool slightly before serving.
Slice the za'atar flatbreads into wedges or squares and serve warm as a delicious appetizer or side dish.

Enjoy your homemade za'atar flatbread with its aromatic flavors and crispy texture!

Labneh (Yogurt Cheese)

Ingredients:

- 32 ounces (about 4 cups) plain Greek yogurt or regular yogurt
- 1 teaspoon salt (optional)
- Olive oil, for drizzling (optional)
- Fresh herbs (such as parsley, mint, or dill), for garnish (optional)
- Za'atar spice blend, for sprinkling (optional)

Instructions:

> Place a large piece of cheesecloth or a clean kitchen towel over a large bowl.
> Pour the yogurt into the center of the cheesecloth.
> Gather the edges of the cheesecloth and tie them together to form a bundle, securing the yogurt inside.
> Hang the bundle over the bowl or place it in a strainer set over the bowl.
> Allow the yogurt to drain in the refrigerator for 12-24 hours, depending on how thick you want your labneh to be. The longer you drain it, the thicker it will become.
> Once the labneh has reached your desired consistency, remove it from the cheesecloth and transfer it to a serving bowl.
> If desired, stir in salt to taste for seasoning.
> Drizzle olive oil over the top of the labneh and garnish with fresh herbs and a sprinkle of za'atar spice blend, if desired.
> Serve the labneh as a dip with pita bread, vegetables, or crackers, or use it as a spread on sandwiches or wraps.
> Store any leftover labneh in an airtight container in the refrigerator for up to one week.

Enjoy your homemade labneh, a delicious and versatile addition to your culinary repertoire!

Mujadara (Lentils and Rice with Caramelized Onions)

Ingredients:

- 1 cup brown or green lentils
- 1 cup basmati rice (or any long-grain rice)
- 3 large onions, thinly sliced
- 1/4 cup olive oil, divided
- 4 cups water or vegetable broth
- 1 teaspoon ground cumin
- 1/2 teaspoon ground coriander
- 1/2 teaspoon ground cinnamon
- Salt and black pepper, to taste
- Fresh parsley, chopped, for garnish (optional)

Instructions:

Rinse the lentils under cold water in a fine-mesh sieve. Drain well and set aside.

In a large pot or saucepan, heat 2 tablespoons of olive oil over medium heat. Add the sliced onions and cook, stirring occasionally, until they are deeply caramelized and golden brown, about 20-25 minutes. Stirring occasionally to prevent burning.

While the onions are caramelizing, in another pot, heat the remaining 2 tablespoons of olive oil over medium heat. Add the rinsed lentils and sauté for a few minutes until they are coated with oil.

Add the water or vegetable broth to the pot with the lentils. Bring to a boil, then reduce the heat to low, cover, and simmer for about 20-25 minutes, or until the lentils are tender but not mushy.

Once the lentils are cooked, add the rice to the pot. Stir well, then cover and cook for another 15-20 minutes, or until the rice is cooked and fluffy and has absorbed all the liquid.

While the rice and lentils are cooking, add the ground cumin, ground coriander, ground cinnamon, salt, and black pepper to the caramelized onions. Stir well to combine and cook for another minute to allow the spices to become fragrant.

Once the rice and lentils are cooked, remove the pot from the heat. Add about half of the caramelized onions to the pot, reserving the rest for garnish.

Gently mix the onions into the rice and lentil mixture until evenly distributed.

Transfer the mujadara to a serving platter or individual plates. Top with the remaining caramelized onions and chopped fresh parsley, if desired.

Serve the mujadara warm as a hearty and satisfying main dish or side dish.

Enjoy your homemade mujadara with its delicious combination of flavors and textures!

Lebanese Fattoush Salad

Ingredients:

For the salad:

- 2 large tomatoes, diced
- 1 cucumber, diced
- 1 red bell pepper, diced
- 1 green bell pepper, diced
- 1 small red onion, thinly sliced
- 2 cups chopped romaine lettuce
- 1 cup chopped fresh parsley
- 1/2 cup chopped fresh mint leaves
- 1 cup chopped radishes
- 1 cup chopped green onions (scallions)
- 1 cup chopped purslane (optional, but traditional)
- 1 cup chopped fresh basil leaves (optional)
- 1 cup chopped fresh cilantro (optional)

For the dressing:

- 1/4 cup extra virgin olive oil
- 3 tablespoons freshly squeezed lemon juice
- 1-2 cloves garlic, minced
- 1 teaspoon ground sumac
- 1 teaspoon ground cumin
- Salt and black pepper, to taste

For the pita chips:

- 2 large pita bread rounds
- 2 tablespoons olive oil
- 1 teaspoon ground sumac
- Salt, to taste

Instructions:

Preheat your oven to 375°F (190°C).
Cut the pita bread rounds into wedges or bite-sized pieces.

Place the pita pieces on a baking sheet. Drizzle with olive oil and sprinkle with sumac and salt. Toss to coat evenly.

Bake the pita chips in the preheated oven for about 10-12 minutes, or until golden brown and crispy. Remove from the oven and let cool.

In a large mixing bowl, combine the diced tomatoes, diced cucumber, diced red and green bell peppers, thinly sliced red onion, chopped romaine lettuce, chopped fresh parsley, chopped fresh mint leaves, chopped radishes, chopped green onions, purslane (if using), chopped fresh basil (if using), and chopped fresh cilantro (if using).

In a small bowl, whisk together the extra virgin olive oil, lemon juice, minced garlic, ground sumac, ground cumin, salt, and black pepper to make the dressing.

Pour the dressing over the salad and toss gently to coat all the ingredients evenly.

Just before serving, add the baked pita chips to the salad and toss gently to combine.

Taste the salad and adjust the seasoning, adding more salt, lemon juice, or spices if needed.

Serve the Lebanese Fattoush salad immediately, allowing the flavors to meld together.

Enjoy your homemade Lebanese Fattoush salad, bursting with fresh flavors and textures!

Turkish Imam Bayildi (Stuffed Eggplant)

Ingredients:

- 4 small to medium-sized eggplants
- Salt, for sweating the eggplants
- 1/4 cup olive oil, plus extra for brushing
- 1 large onion, finely chopped
- 3 cloves garlic, minced
- 2 large tomatoes, diced
- 2 tablespoons tomato paste
- 1 teaspoon sugar
- 1 teaspoon ground cumin
- 1/2 teaspoon paprika
- Salt and black pepper, to taste
- 1/4 cup chopped fresh parsley, plus extra for garnish
- 1/4 cup chopped fresh mint, plus extra for garnish
- Juice of 1 lemon
- Optional: crumbled feta cheese, for serving

Instructions:

Preheat your oven to 375°F (190°C).

Slice the eggplants in half lengthwise, leaving the stems intact. Score the flesh of each eggplant half in a crisscross pattern, being careful not to cut through the skin. This will help the eggplants cook evenly and absorb the flavors of the stuffing.

Sprinkle the cut sides of the eggplants with salt and let them sit for about 15-20 minutes to release any bitterness. After 15-20 minutes, pat the eggplants dry with paper towels to remove excess moisture.

Heat 1/4 cup of olive oil in a large skillet over medium heat. Add the chopped onion and minced garlic, and sauté until softened and translucent, about 5-7 minutes.

Add the diced tomatoes, tomato paste, sugar, ground cumin, paprika, salt, and black pepper to the skillet. Cook for another 5 minutes, stirring occasionally, until the tomatoes break down and the mixture thickens slightly.

Stir in the chopped fresh parsley and chopped fresh mint. Cook for another minute, then remove the skillet from the heat.

Place the eggplant halves in a baking dish, cut side up. Brush the cut sides of the eggplants with olive oil.

Spoon the tomato mixture evenly over the cut sides of the eggplants, pressing down gently to pack the stuffing.

Cover the baking dish with aluminum foil and bake the stuffed eggplants in the preheated oven for about 30-40 minutes, or until the eggplants are tender and cooked through.

Remove the foil from the baking dish and bake for an additional 10-15 minutes, or until the tops are lightly browned and caramelized.

Remove the stuffed eggplants from the oven and let them cool slightly.

Garnish the Turkish Imam Bayildi with chopped fresh parsley and chopped fresh mint. Drizzle with lemon juice.

Serve the stuffed eggplants warm, optionally topped with crumbled feta cheese.

Enjoy your delicious homemade Turkish Imam Bayildi, a flavorful and satisfying dish!

Moroccan Couscous with Roasted Vegetables

Ingredients:

For the roasted vegetables:

- 2 medium carrots, peeled and cut into chunks
- 1 large sweet potato, peeled and cut into chunks
- 1 red bell pepper, seeded and cut into chunks
- 1 yellow bell pepper, seeded and cut into chunks
- 1 red onion, cut into chunks
- 2 tablespoons olive oil
- 1 teaspoon ground cumin
- 1 teaspoon ground coriander
- 1/2 teaspoon smoked paprika
- Salt and black pepper, to taste

For the couscous:

- 1 1/2 cups couscous
- 1 3/4 cups vegetable broth or water
- 2 tablespoons olive oil
- 1 teaspoon ground cumin
- 1 teaspoon ground coriander
- 1/2 teaspoon ground cinnamon
- 1/4 teaspoon ground ginger
- Salt and black pepper, to taste
- 1/4 cup chopped fresh parsley, for garnish
- Lemon wedges, for serving (optional)

Instructions:

Preheat your oven to 400°F (200°C). Line a baking sheet with parchment paper or aluminum foil.

In a large mixing bowl, toss together the carrot chunks, sweet potato chunks, red bell pepper chunks, yellow bell pepper chunks, and red onion chunks with olive oil, ground cumin, ground coriander, smoked paprika, salt, and black pepper until evenly coated.

Spread the seasoned vegetables in a single layer on the prepared baking sheet.

Roast the vegetables in the preheated oven for about 25-30 minutes, or until they are tender and caramelized, stirring halfway through cooking.

While the vegetables are roasting, prepare the couscous. In a medium saucepan, bring the vegetable broth or water to a boil.

Stir in the couscous, olive oil, ground cumin, ground coriander, ground cinnamon, ground ginger, salt, and black pepper.

Remove the saucepan from the heat, cover, and let the couscous sit for about 5 minutes, or until all the liquid is absorbed.

Fluff the couscous with a fork to separate the grains.

Once the roasted vegetables are done, remove them from the oven and let them cool slightly.

To serve, spoon the couscous onto a serving platter or individual plates. Arrange the roasted vegetables on top of the couscous.

Garnish the Moroccan couscous with chopped fresh parsley.

Serve the couscous with lemon wedges on the side for squeezing over the dish, if desired.

Enjoy your flavorful Moroccan couscous with roasted vegetables as a satisfying and nutritious meal!

Persian Sabzi Polo (Herb Rice)

Ingredients:

- 2 cups basmati rice
- 4 cups water
- 1 teaspoon salt
- 2 tablespoons vegetable oil or ghee

For the herb mixture:

- 2 cups chopped mixed herbs (such as parsley, cilantro, dill, and green onions)
- 1 tablespoon vegetable oil
- 2 cloves garlic, minced
- 1 teaspoon ground turmeric
- 1/2 teaspoon ground cumin
- 1/2 teaspoon ground cinnamon
- Salt and black pepper, to taste

Instructions:

Rinse the basmati rice under cold water until the water runs clear. Drain well.
In a large pot, bring 4 cups of water to a boil. Add 1 teaspoon of salt to the boiling water.
Stir in the rinsed basmati rice and cook for about 6-7 minutes, or until the rice is partially cooked. It should still have a firm texture. Drain the rice and set aside.
In a large skillet or frying pan, heat 1 tablespoon of vegetable oil over medium heat. Add the minced garlic and sauté for about 1 minute, until fragrant.
Add the chopped mixed herbs to the skillet and cook for another 3-4 minutes, stirring occasionally, until the herbs are wilted and fragrant.
Stir in the ground turmeric, ground cumin, ground cinnamon, salt, and black pepper. Cook for another minute to toast the spices.
Add the partially cooked rice to the skillet with the herb mixture. Gently toss everything together until the rice is evenly coated with the herbs and spices.
Reduce the heat to low. Cover the skillet with a tight-fitting lid and let the rice cook for about 15-20 minutes, or until the rice is fully cooked and tender.
Once the rice is cooked, remove the skillet from the heat and let it sit, covered, for another 5 minutes to steam.
Fluff the Persian Sabzi Polo with a fork to separate the grains.
Transfer the Sabzi Polo to a serving platter and serve hot as a flavorful and aromatic side dish.

Enjoy your homemade Persian Sabzi Polo, a delicious and fragrant herb rice that pairs well with a variety of main dishes!

Stuffed Zucchini with Rice and Pine Nuts

Ingredients:

- 4 medium zucchini
- 1 cup long-grain rice (such as basmati)
- 2 cups vegetable broth or water
- 1/4 cup pine nuts
- 1 small onion, finely chopped
- 2 cloves garlic, minced
- 1/2 cup chopped fresh parsley
- 1/4 cup chopped fresh dill
- 1/4 cup chopped fresh mint
- 1 teaspoon ground cumin
- 1/2 teaspoon ground cinnamon
- Salt and black pepper, to taste
- 2 tablespoons olive oil, plus extra for drizzling
- Lemon wedges, for serving (optional)
- Greek yogurt or tzatziki, for serving (optional)

Instructions:

Preheat your oven to 375°F (190°C). Grease a baking dish with olive oil or cooking spray.
Cut the zucchini in half lengthwise. Use a spoon to carefully scoop out the seeds and flesh from the center of each zucchini half, leaving about 1/4 inch of flesh along the edges. Reserve the scooped-out flesh.
Rinse the rice under cold water until the water runs clear. Drain well.
In a medium saucepan, bring the vegetable broth or water to a boil. Stir in the rinsed rice, reduce the heat to low, cover, and simmer for about 15-20 minutes, or until the rice is cooked and the liquid is absorbed.
While the rice is cooking, heat 2 tablespoons of olive oil in a large skillet over medium heat. Add the chopped onion and minced garlic, and sauté until softened and translucent, about 5 minutes.
Chop the reserved zucchini flesh and add it to the skillet with the onions and garlic. Cook for another 3-4 minutes, until the zucchini is tender.
Stir in the pine nuts, chopped fresh parsley, chopped fresh dill, chopped fresh mint, ground cumin, ground cinnamon, salt, and black pepper. Cook for another 2-3 minutes to toast the pine nuts and blend the flavors.
Once the rice is cooked, add it to the skillet with the herb mixture. Stir well to combine all the ingredients.
Fill each hollowed-out zucchini half with the rice and herb mixture, pressing down gently to pack the filling.

Arrange the stuffed zucchini halves in the prepared baking dish. Drizzle with a little extra olive oil.

Cover the baking dish with aluminum foil and bake the stuffed zucchini in the preheated oven for about 30-35 minutes, or until the zucchini is tender.

Remove the foil from the baking dish and bake for an additional 5-10 minutes, or until the tops are lightly golden.

Serve the stuffed zucchini hot, optionally with lemon wedges on the side for squeezing over the zucchini. You can also serve them with a dollop of Greek yogurt or tzatziki on top.

Enjoy your delicious homemade stuffed zucchini with rice and pine nuts as a satisfying and flavorful meal!

Turkish Bulgur Pilaf with Chickpeas and Tomatoes

Ingredients:

- 1 cup bulgur wheat
- 1 3/4 cups vegetable broth or water
- 1 tablespoon olive oil
- 1 small onion, finely chopped
- 2 cloves garlic, minced
- 1 teaspoon ground cumin
- 1 teaspoon ground coriander
- 1/2 teaspoon paprika
- 1/2 teaspoon ground cinnamon
- 1 can (15 ounces) chickpeas, drained and rinsed
- 1 can (14.5 ounces) diced tomatoes, undrained
- Salt and black pepper, to taste
- Fresh parsley, chopped, for garnish
- Lemon wedges, for serving (optional)

Instructions:

Rinse the bulgur wheat under cold water until the water runs clear. Drain well.

In a medium saucepan, heat the olive oil over medium heat. Add the chopped onion and minced garlic, and sauté until softened and translucent, about 5 minutes.

Stir in the ground cumin, ground coriander, paprika, and ground cinnamon. Cook for another minute to toast the spices and release their flavors.

Add the drained and rinsed chickpeas to the saucepan, along with the diced tomatoes (with their juices) and the rinsed bulgur wheat. Stir well to combine.

Pour the vegetable broth or water over the bulgur mixture and season with salt and black pepper, to taste. Stir again to combine.

Bring the mixture to a boil, then reduce the heat to low. Cover the saucepan with a tight-fitting lid and simmer for about 15-20 minutes, or until the bulgur is tender and has absorbed all the liquid.

Once the bulgur is cooked, remove the saucepan from the heat. Fluff the bulgur pilaf with a fork to separate the grains.

Transfer the bulgur pilaf to a serving dish and garnish with chopped fresh parsley.

Serve the Turkish Bulgur Pilaf with Chickpeas and Tomatoes hot, optionally with lemon wedges on the side for squeezing over the pilaf.

Enjoy your flavorful and nutritious Turkish Bulgur Pilaf with Chickpeas and Tomatoes as a delicious main dish or side dish!

Egyptian Kushari (Rice, Lentils, and Pasta)

Ingredients:

For the kushari:

- 1 cup white rice
- 1 cup brown lentils
- 1 cup dried elbow macaroni or penne pasta
- 3 tablespoons vegetable oil
- Salt, to taste

For the tomato sauce:

- 1 can (14.5 ounces) diced tomatoes
- 2 cloves garlic, minced
- 1 tablespoon tomato paste
- 1 teaspoon ground cumin
- 1 teaspoon ground coriander
- 1/2 teaspoon ground cinnamon
- 1/4 teaspoon cayenne pepper (optional)
- Salt and black pepper, to taste
- 1 tablespoon olive oil

For the fried onions:

- 1 large onion, thinly sliced
- Vegetable oil, for frying

Instructions:

Rinse the white rice and brown lentils separately under cold water until the water runs clear. Drain well.

In a medium saucepan, combine the white rice with 2 cups of water and a pinch of salt. Bring to a boil, then reduce the heat to low, cover, and simmer for about 15-20 minutes, or until the rice is cooked and the water is absorbed.

In another medium saucepan, combine the brown lentils with 2 cups of water and a pinch of salt. Bring to a boil, then reduce the heat to low, cover, and simmer for about 20-25 minutes, or until the lentils are tender but not mushy. Drain any excess water.

Cook the elbow macaroni or penne pasta according to the package instructions until al dente. Drain and set aside.

To make the tomato sauce, heat olive oil in a saucepan over medium heat. Add minced garlic and sauté until fragrant, about 1 minute.

Add diced tomatoes, tomato paste, ground cumin, ground coriander, ground cinnamon, cayenne pepper (if using), salt, and black pepper. Stir well to combine.

Bring the tomato sauce to a simmer and cook for about 10-15 minutes, stirring occasionally, until the sauce has thickened slightly. Remove from heat and set aside.

To make the fried onions, heat vegetable oil in a deep skillet or frying pan over medium-high heat. Add thinly sliced onions and fry until golden brown and crispy, stirring occasionally. Remove the fried onions from the oil and drain on paper towels.

In a large mixing bowl, combine the cooked rice, lentils, and pasta. Drizzle with vegetable oil and toss gently to combine. Season with salt to taste.

To serve, spoon the rice, lentil, and pasta mixture onto individual serving plates. Top with a generous spoonful of the tomato sauce and a sprinkling of crispy fried onions.

Serve the Egyptian Kushari hot, optionally with additional tomato sauce and fried onions on the side.

Enjoy your homemade Egyptian Kushari, a comforting and flavorful dish that's perfect for sharing with family and friends!

Muhammara Stuffed Mushrooms

Ingredients:

- 16 large mushrooms, cleaned with stems removed
- 1 cup muhammara dip (store-bought or homemade, see below for a basic recipe)
- 1/4 cup breadcrumbs
- 2 tablespoons olive oil
- Salt and pepper, to taste
- Fresh parsley, chopped, for garnish (optional)

For the muhammara dip:

- 2 large red bell peppers
- 1 cup walnuts, toasted
- 1/4 cup breadcrumbs
- 2 cloves garlic, minced
- 2 tablespoons lemon juice
- 2 tablespoons olive oil
- 1 tablespoon pomegranate molasses
- 1 teaspoon ground cumin
- 1/2 teaspoon smoked paprika
- Salt, to taste

Instructions:

Preheat your oven to 375°F (190°C). Line a baking sheet with parchment paper.
Prepare the muhammara dip: Preheat the broiler in your oven. Place the red bell peppers on the baking sheet and broil, turning occasionally, until charred and blistered on all sides, about 15-20 minutes. Remove from the oven and transfer the peppers to a bowl. Cover the bowl with plastic wrap and let the peppers steam for about 10 minutes. Once cooled, remove the skins, stems, and seeds from the peppers.
In a food processor, combine the roasted red peppers, toasted walnuts, breadcrumbs, minced garlic, lemon juice, olive oil, pomegranate molasses, ground cumin, smoked paprika, and salt. Blend until smooth, adding a little water if needed to achieve your desired consistency. Taste and adjust seasoning if necessary. Transfer the muhammara dip to a bowl and set aside.
In a small bowl, mix together the breadcrumbs and olive oil until well combined.
Stuff each mushroom cap with a spoonful of muhammara dip, pressing down gently to fill the cavity.
Place the stuffed mushrooms on the prepared baking sheet. Sprinkle the breadcrumb mixture over the tops of the stuffed mushrooms.

Bake the stuffed mushrooms in the preheated oven for about 15-20 minutes, or until the mushrooms are tender and the breadcrumbs are golden brown.
Remove the stuffed mushrooms from the oven and let them cool slightly before serving.
Garnish with chopped fresh parsley, if desired, before serving.

Enjoy your muhammara stuffed mushrooms as a flavorful appetizer or snack!

Lebanese Mujadara with Cucumber Yogurt Salad

Ingredients for Mujadara:

For the Mujadara:

- 1 cup brown or green lentils
- 1 cup basmati rice
- 3 large onions, thinly sliced
- 1/4 cup olive oil
- 1 teaspoon ground cumin
- 1/2 teaspoon ground cinnamon
- Salt and black pepper, to taste
- Water or vegetable broth, as needed

For the Cucumber Yogurt Salad:

- 1 large cucumber, diced
- 1 cup plain Greek yogurt
- 2 cloves garlic, minced
- 2 tablespoons chopped fresh mint
- 1 tablespoon lemon juice
- Salt and black pepper, to taste

Instructions:

Rinse the lentils under cold water in a fine-mesh sieve. Drain well and set aside.

In a large skillet or frying pan, heat the olive oil over medium heat. Add the thinly sliced onions and cook, stirring occasionally, until they are deeply caramelized and golden brown, about 20-25 minutes. Stirring occasionally to prevent burning.

While the onions are caramelizing, cook the lentils. In a medium saucepan, combine the rinsed lentils with water or vegetable broth, enough to cover the lentils by about 2 inches. Bring to a boil, then reduce the heat to low, cover, and simmer for about 20-25 minutes, or until the lentils are tender but not mushy. Drain any excess liquid.

In a separate saucepan, cook the basmati rice according to package instructions. You can use water or vegetable broth for extra flavor.

Once the lentils and rice are cooked, combine them in a large bowl. Season with ground cumin, ground cinnamon, salt, and black pepper. Stir well to combine.

Add about half of the caramelized onions to the lentil and rice mixture, reserving the rest for garnish. Stir to incorporate the onions.

To make the cucumber yogurt salad, in a separate bowl, combine diced cucumber, plain Greek yogurt, minced garlic, chopped fresh mint, lemon juice, salt, and black pepper. Mix well to combine.

Serve the Mujadara warm, topped with the remaining caramelized onions and accompanied by the cucumber yogurt salad.

Enjoy your Mujadara with Cucumber Yogurt Salad as a delicious and satisfying meal!

Feel free to adjust the seasoning and ingredients according to your taste preferences.

Persian Kashk-e Bademjan (Eggplant Dip)

Ingredients:

- 2 large eggplants
- 2 tablespoons olive oil, plus extra for drizzling
- 1 large onion, finely chopped
- 3 cloves garlic, minced
- 1/4 teaspoon ground turmeric
- Salt and black pepper, to taste
- 1/4 cup kashk (fermented whey), or substitute with Greek yogurt or sour cream
- Chopped fresh mint or parsley, for garnish (optional)

Instructions:

Preheat your oven to 400°F (200°C).

Prick the eggplants with a fork or knife in several places. This allows steam to escape during roasting.

Place the eggplants on a baking sheet lined with parchment paper or aluminum foil. Drizzle with a little olive oil and rub to coat evenly.

Roast the eggplants in the preheated oven for about 40-45 minutes, or until the skin is charred and the flesh is soft and tender. Turn the eggplants occasionally during roasting to ensure even cooking.

Remove the eggplants from the oven and let them cool slightly. Once cool enough to handle, peel off the charred skin and discard.

In a large skillet or frying pan, heat 2 tablespoons of olive oil over medium heat. Add the finely chopped onion and cook, stirring occasionally, until caramelized and golden brown, about 10-15 minutes.

Add the minced garlic and ground turmeric to the skillet with the caramelized onions. Cook for another minute, until fragrant.

Add the roasted eggplant flesh to the skillet, breaking it up with a spoon. Stir well to combine with the caramelized onions, garlic, and turmeric.

Season the mixture with salt and black pepper, to taste. Cook for another 2-3 minutes to allow the flavors to meld.

Transfer the mixture to a serving dish. Drizzle the kashk (or substitute) over the top. Garnish with chopped fresh mint or parsley, if desired.

Serve the Kashk-e Bademjan warm or at room temperature, accompanied by flatbread or pita bread for dipping.

Enjoy your homemade Kashk-e Bademjan as a delicious and authentic Persian appetizer!

Moroccan Chickpea Tagine with Apricots and Almonds

Ingredients:

- 2 tablespoons olive oil
- 1 large onion, diced
- 3 cloves garlic, minced
- 1 teaspoon ground cumin
- 1 teaspoon ground coriander
- 1 teaspoon ground cinnamon
- 1/2 teaspoon ground turmeric
- 1/4 teaspoon ground ginger
- 1/4 teaspoon cayenne pepper (optional, for heat)
- 1 can (15 ounces) chickpeas, drained and rinsed
- 1 can (14.5 ounces) diced tomatoes, undrained
- 1/2 cup dried apricots, chopped
- 1/4 cup sliced almonds
- Salt and black pepper, to taste
- Fresh cilantro or parsley, chopped, for garnish (optional)
- Cooked couscous or rice, for serving

Instructions:

Heat the olive oil in a large skillet or tagine over medium heat. Add the diced onion and cook until softened and translucent, about 5 minutes.
Add the minced garlic to the skillet and cook for another minute until fragrant.
Stir in the ground cumin, ground coriander, ground cinnamon, ground turmeric, ground ginger, and cayenne pepper (if using). Cook for another minute to toast the spices.
Add the drained and rinsed chickpeas to the skillet, along with the diced tomatoes (with their juices). Stir to combine.
Bring the mixture to a simmer and let it cook for about 10-15 minutes, stirring occasionally, to allow the flavors to meld together and the sauce to thicken slightly.
Stir in the chopped dried apricots and sliced almonds. Cook for another 5 minutes, or until the apricots are softened and the almonds are toasted.
Season the tagine with salt and black pepper, to taste. Adjust the seasoning if necessary.
Serve the Moroccan Chickpea Tagine with Apricots and Almonds hot, garnished with chopped fresh cilantro or parsley, if desired. Serve over cooked couscous or rice.

Enjoy your flavorful and aromatic Moroccan Chickpea Tagine with Apricots and Almonds as a hearty and satisfying meal!

Lebanese Foul Mudammas (Fava Beans)

Ingredients:

- 2 cups cooked fava beans (canned or dried and cooked)
- 2 cloves garlic, minced
- 1/4 cup chopped fresh parsley
- 1/4 cup chopped fresh mint
- 1 small red onion, finely chopped
- 1 tomato, diced
- 2 tablespoons lemon juice
- 2 tablespoons olive oil
- Salt, to taste
- Black pepper, to taste
- Optional toppings: chopped green onions, diced cucumber, pickled turnips, tahini sauce, or crumbled feta cheese

Instructions:

If using dried fava beans, soak them overnight in water. Drain and rinse the soaked fava beans, then cook them in a pot of boiling water until tender, about 45 minutes to 1 hour. If using canned fava beans, simply drain and rinse them.

In a large mixing bowl, combine the cooked fava beans, minced garlic, chopped parsley, chopped mint, finely chopped red onion, and diced tomato.

Drizzle the lemon juice and olive oil over the fava bean mixture. Season with salt and black pepper, to taste.

Gently toss all the ingredients together until well combined.

Taste and adjust the seasoning, adding more lemon juice, salt, or black pepper if desired.

Serve the Lebanese Foul Mudammas in individual bowls, topped with optional toppings such as chopped green onions, diced cucumber, pickled turnips, tahini sauce, or crumbled feta cheese.

Enjoy your Lebanese Foul Mudammas as a delicious and nutritious breakfast or snack, served with warm pita bread or flatbread on the side.

This dish is versatile, so feel free to adjust the ingredients and seasonings according to your taste preferences.

Turkish Red Lentil Soup (Mercimek Çorbası)

Ingredients:

- 1 cup red lentils, rinsed and drained
- 1 onion, chopped
- 2 carrots, chopped
- 2 cloves garlic, minced
- 1 tablespoon tomato paste
- 1 teaspoon ground cumin
- 1 teaspoon paprika
- 1/2 teaspoon ground turmeric
- 6 cups vegetable broth or water
- Salt and black pepper, to taste
- Juice of 1 lemon
- Olive oil, for drizzling (optional)
- Chopped fresh parsley or mint, for garnish (optional)
- Crusty bread, for serving

Instructions:

In a large pot, heat a little olive oil over medium heat. Add the chopped onion and carrots, and cook until softened, about 5 minutes.

Add the minced garlic, tomato paste, ground cumin, paprika, and ground turmeric to the pot Stir well to combine and cook for another minute, until fragrant.

Add the rinsed red lentils to the pot, followed by the vegetable broth or water. Stir to combine.

Bring the soup to a boil, then reduce the heat to low. Cover and simmer for about 20-25 minutes, or until the lentils and vegetables are soft and cooked through.

Using an immersion blender or a regular blender, puree the soup until smooth and creamy. If using a regular blender, be sure to blend in batches and vent the lid to avoid steam build-up.

Season the soup with salt and black pepper, to taste. Stir in the lemon juice.

Ladle the Turkish Red Lentil Soup into bowls. Drizzle with a little olive oil, if desired, and garnish with chopped fresh parsley or mint.

Serve the soup hot, accompanied by crusty bread for dipping.

Enjoy your homemade Turkish Red Lentil Soup, a comforting and nutritious dish that's perfect for chilly days!

Persian Borani Esfenaj (Spinach Yogurt Dip)

Ingredients:

- 1 lb (450g) fresh spinach leaves, washed and chopped
- 1 large onion, finely chopped
- 2 cloves garlic, minced
- 1 tablespoon olive oil
- 1 cup plain Greek yogurt
- 1 teaspoon ground turmeric
- Salt and black pepper, to taste
- 1 tablespoon butter or ghee (optional, for garnish)
- Chopped walnuts or fried onions, for garnish (optional)

Instructions:

Heat olive oil in a large skillet over medium heat. Add chopped onion and minced garlic, and sauté until softened and golden brown, about 5-7 minutes.
Add chopped spinach to the skillet and cook until wilted, stirring occasionally, about 5 minutes.
Once the spinach is cooked, remove the skillet from heat and let the mixture cool slightly.
In a mixing bowl, combine the cooked spinach mixture with Greek yogurt, ground turmeric, salt, and black pepper. Stir well to combine.
Transfer the Borani Esfenaj to a serving dish.
In a small saucepan, melt butter or ghee over medium heat. Once melted, cook until the butter turns golden brown and develops a nutty aroma, about 2-3 minutes. Be careful not to burn it.
Drizzle the browned butter or ghee over the Borani Esfenaj.
Optionally, garnish the Borani Esfenaj with chopped walnuts or fried onions.
Serve the Borani Esfenaj as a dip or side dish, accompanied by flatbread or pita bread.

Enjoy your Borani Esfenaj, a delicious and nutritious Persian spinach yogurt dip!

Lebanese Batata Harra (Spicy Potatoes)

Ingredients:

- 4 large potatoes, peeled and cut into small cubes
- 3 tablespoons olive oil
- 4 cloves garlic, minced
- 1 red chili pepper, finely chopped (adjust to taste)
- 1 teaspoon ground coriander
- 1 teaspoon ground cumin
- 1/2 teaspoon paprika
- 1/4 teaspoon cayenne pepper (optional, for extra heat)
- Salt, to taste
- Juice of 1 lemon
- Fresh cilantro or parsley, chopped, for garnish

Instructions:

Heat 2 tablespoons of olive oil in a large skillet over medium-high heat.
Add the cubed potatoes to the skillet and cook, stirring occasionally, until they are golden brown and crispy on the outside and tender on the inside, about 15-20 minutes. You may need to adjust the heat to prevent burning.
Once the potatoes are cooked, transfer them to a plate and set aside.
In the same skillet, add the remaining 1 tablespoon of olive oil.
Add the minced garlic and chopped red chili pepper to the skillet. Sauté for 1-2 minutes until fragrant.
Stir in the ground coriander, ground cumin, paprika, cayenne pepper (if using), and salt. Cook for another minute to toast the spices.
Return the cooked potatoes to the skillet and toss well to coat them evenly with the spicy mixture.
Cook for an additional 2-3 minutes to allow the flavors to meld together.
Remove the skillet from heat and drizzle the lemon juice over the potatoes. Toss to combine.
Transfer the Batata Harra to a serving dish and garnish with chopped fresh cilantro or parsley.
Serve the Lebanese Batata Harra hot as a delicious side dish or appetizer.

Enjoy your flavorful and spicy Lebanese Batata Harra! Adjust the amount of chili pepper according to your desired level of spiciness.

Moroccan Vegetable Tagine with Couscous

Ingredients:

For the Vegetable Tagine:

- 2 tablespoons olive oil
- 1 onion, chopped
- 2 cloves garlic, minced
- 1 teaspoon ground cumin
- 1 teaspoon ground coriander
- 1/2 teaspoon ground cinnamon
- 1/2 teaspoon ground ginger
- 1/4 teaspoon ground turmeric
- Pinch of saffron threads (optional)
- 1 can (14.5 ounces) diced tomatoes, undrained
- 1 cup vegetable broth
- 2 carrots, peeled and sliced
- 2 zucchinis, sliced
- 1 bell pepper, chopped
- 1 cup cauliflower florets
- 1 cup chickpeas (cooked or canned, drained and rinsed)
- Salt and black pepper, to taste
- Fresh cilantro or parsley, chopped, for garnish

For the Couscous:

- 1 cup couscous
- 1 cup vegetable broth or water
- 1 tablespoon olive oil
- Salt, to taste

Instructions:

Heat olive oil in a large skillet or tagine over medium heat. Add chopped onion and minced garlic, and cook until softened, about 5 minutes.
Add ground cumin, ground coriander, ground cinnamon, ground ginger, ground turmeric, and saffron threads (if using) to the skillet. Cook for another minute until fragrant.
Stir in diced tomatoes and vegetable broth. Bring the mixture to a simmer.

Add sliced carrots, sliced zucchinis, chopped bell pepper, cauliflower florets, and chickpeas to the skillet. Stir to combine.

Cover the skillet and let the vegetable tagine simmer for about 20-25 minutes, or until the vegetables are tender, stirring occasionally. If the sauce becomes too thick, you can add a little more vegetable broth or water.

While the vegetable tagine is simmering, prepare the couscous. In a separate pot, bring vegetable broth or water to a boil. Stir in couscous, olive oil, and salt. Remove from heat, cover, and let it sit for about 5 minutes, until the couscous absorbs the liquid. Fluff the couscous with a fork.

Taste the vegetable tagine and adjust the seasoning with salt and black pepper, if needed.

Serve the Moroccan Vegetable Tagine hot, spooned over the fluffy couscous. Garnish with chopped fresh cilantro or parsley before serving.

Enjoy your flavorful Moroccan Vegetable Tagine with Couscous as a satisfying and nutritious meal!

Turkish Börek with Spinach and Feta

Ingredients:

For the filling:

- 2 tablespoons olive oil
- 1 onion, finely chopped
- 3 cloves garlic, minced
- 1 lb (450g) fresh spinach leaves, washed and chopped
- Salt and black pepper, to taste
- 1 teaspoon ground cumin
- 1 teaspoon paprika
- 1/2 teaspoon ground nutmeg
- 1/2 teaspoon red pepper flakes (optional)
- 8 oz (225g) feta cheese, crumbled
- 1/4 cup chopped fresh parsley
- 1/4 cup chopped fresh dill (optional)

For the börek:

- 1 lb (450g) phyllo dough, thawed if frozen
- 1/2 cup unsalted butter, melted
- 1 egg, beaten (for egg wash)
- Sesame seeds or nigella seeds, for topping (optional)

Instructions:

Preheat your oven to 375°F (190°C). Grease a baking dish with butter or oil.
Heat olive oil in a large skillet over medium heat. Add chopped onion and minced garlic, and sauté until softened, about 5 minutes.
Add chopped spinach to the skillet and cook until wilted, stirring occasionally, about 3-5 minutes. Season with salt, black pepper, ground cumin, paprika, nutmeg, and red pepper flakes (if using). Stir well to combine.
Remove the skillet from heat and let the spinach mixture cool slightly.
In a mixing bowl, combine the cooked spinach mixture with crumbled feta cheese, chopped fresh parsley, and chopped fresh dill (if using). Mix well to combine.
Unroll the phyllo dough and cover it with a damp towel to prevent it from drying out.
Take one sheet of phyllo dough and place it on a clean work surface. Brush it lightly with melted butter. Repeat with another sheet of phyllo dough, stacking it on top of the first sheet. Continue until you have 4-5 layers of phyllo dough.

Spoon a portion of the spinach and feta mixture along one edge of the phyllo dough, leaving about 1 inch of space from the edges. Roll up the phyllo dough tightly to form a log. Transfer the rolled börek to the prepared baking dish, seam side down. Repeat the process with the remaining phyllo dough and filing until you have used up all the filling.

Brush the tops of the börek with beaten egg and sprinkle with sesame seeds or nigella seeds, if desired.

Bake the börek in the preheated oven for about 25-30 minutes, or until golden brown and crispy.

Remove the börek from the oven and let it cool slightly before slicing and serving.

Enjoy your delicious Turkish Börek with Spinach and Feta as a flavorful appetizer, snack, or light meal!

Persian Jeweled Rice (Javaher Polow)

Ingredients:

- 2 cups basmati rice
- 4 cups water
- 1 teaspoon salt
- 1/4 teaspoon ground saffron (dissolved in 2 tablespoons hot water)
- 3 tablespoons butter or ghee
- 1/2 cup slivered almonds
- 1/2 cup shelled pistachios
- 1/2 cup golden raisins
- 1/2 cup dried cranberries or barberries
- 1/4 teaspoon ground cinnamon
- 1/4 teaspoon ground cardamom
- 1/4 teaspoon ground nutmeg
- 1/4 teaspoon ground cloves
- 1/4 teaspoon ground black pepper
- 1/4 cup orange zest (from 2 oranges), thinly sliced
- 1/4 cup pomegranate seeds, for garnish (optional)
- Fresh parsley or mint, chopped, for garnish (optional)

Instructions:

Rinse the basmati rice under cold water until the water runs clear. Drain well.
In a large pot, bring 4 cups of water to a boil. Add 1 teaspoon of salt to the boiling water.
Add the rinsed basmati rice to the boiling water and cook for about 5-7 minutes, or until the rice is parboiled and slightly tender. Be careful not to overcook the rice.
Drain the parboiled rice in a fine-mesh sieve and rinse it under cold water to stop the cooking process. Set aside.
In a small bowl, dissolve the ground saffron in 2 tablespoons of hot water. Set aside.
In a large non-stick skillet or Dutch oven, melt the butter or ghee over medium heat.
Add the slivered almonds and shelled pistachios to the skillet. Cook, stirring frequently, until the nuts are golden brown and fragrant, about 3-5 minutes.

Add the golden raisins and dried cranberries (or barberries) to the skillet. Cook for another 2-3 minutes, stirring occasionally.

Stir in the ground cinnamon, ground cardamom, ground nutmeg, ground cloves, and ground black pepper. Cook for another minute to toast the spices.

Add the parboiled rice to the skillet, along with the sliced orange zest and dissolved saffron water. Gently toss everything together until the rice is evenly coated with the nuts, fruits, and spices.

Cover the skillet with a tight-fitting lid and reduce the heat to low. Let the rice steam for about 20-25 minutes, or until it's fully cooked and fluffy.

Once the rice is cooked, remove the skillet from heat and let it sit, covered, for 5 minutes.

Fluff the Persian Jeweled Rice with a fork and transfer it to a serving platter.

Garnish the rice with pomegranate seeds (if using) and chopped fresh parsley or mint.

Serve the Persian Jeweled Rice as a colorful and festive side dish alongside your favorite main course.

Enjoy your delicious and aromatic Persian Jeweled Rice!

Stuffed Bell Peppers with Rice and Lentils

Ingredients:

- 4 large bell peppers (any color), tops cut off and seeds removed
- 1 cup cooked brown rice
- 1/2 cup cooked lentils (green or brown)
- 1 onion, finely chopped
- 2 cloves garlic, minced
- 1 carrot, grated
- 1/2 cup diced tomatoes (fresh or canned)
- 1/4 cup chopped fresh parsley or cilantro
- 1 teaspoon ground cumin
- 1 teaspoon paprika
- 1/2 teaspoon dried oregano
- Salt and black pepper, to taste
- 1 cup vegetable broth or water
- Grated cheese (optional, for topping)

Instructions:

Preheat your oven to 375°F (190°C).

In a large skillet, heat a little oil over medium heat. Add the chopped onion and minced garlic, and sauté until softened, about 5 minutes.

Add the grated carrot to the skillet and cook for another 3-4 minutes.

Stir in the cooked brown rice, cooked lentils, diced tomatoes, chopped parsley or cilantro, ground cumin, paprika, dried oregano, salt, and black pepper. Mix well to combine and cook for another 2-3 minutes.

Pour the vegetable broth or water into the skillet and stir to combine. Let the mixture simmer for about 5 minutes, allowing the flavors to meld together. Remove from heat.

Arrange the hollowed-out bell peppers in a baking dish, standing upright.

Carefully stuff each bell pepper with the rice and lentil mixture, pressing down gently to pack the filling.

If desired, top each stuffed bell pepper with grated cheese.

Cover the baking dish with aluminum foil and bake in the preheated oven for about 30-35 minutes, or until the bell peppers are tender.

Remove the foil and bake for an additional 5-10 minutes, or until the cheese is melted and bubbly (if using).

Remove the stuffed bell peppers from the oven and let them cool slightly before serving.
Serve the stuffed bell peppers hot, garnished with additional chopped parsley or cilantro if desired.

Enjoy your delicious Stuffed Bell Peppers with Rice and Lentils as a satisfying and nutritious meal!

Lebanese Tabbouleh Stuffed Avocados

Ingredients:

- 4 ripe avocados
- 1 cup cooked bulgur wheat or quinoa
- 1 cup chopped fresh parsley
- 1/2 cup chopped fresh mint
- 1/2 cup diced tomatoes
- 1/4 cup diced red onion
- 1/4 cup chopped cucumber
- Juice of 1-2 lemons
- 3 tablespoons extra virgin olive oil
- Salt and black pepper, to taste

Instructions:

Cut the avocados in half lengthwise and remove the pits. Scoop out a little bit of the flesh from each avocado half to create a larger cavity for the tabbouleh filling. Reserve the scooped-out avocado flesh for another use.
In a large mixing bowl, combine the cooked bulgur wheat or quinoa, chopped parsley, chopped mint, diced tomatoes, diced red onion, and chopped cucumber.
Drizzle the lemon juice and extra virgin olive oil over the tabbouleh mixture.
Season with salt and black pepper, to taste.
Gently toss all the ingredients together until well combined and evenly coated with the dressing.
Taste and adjust the seasoning, adding more lemon juice, olive oil, salt, or pepper as needed.
Spoon the tabbouleh mixture into the cavity of each avocado half, packing it in lightly and mounding it on top.
Serve the Lebanese Tabbouleh Stuffed Avocados immediately, garnished with additional chopped parsley or mint if desired.
Enjoy your delicious and refreshing Tabbouleh Stuffed Avocados as a light and satisfying appetizer or side dish!

This dish is best served fresh and can be enjoyed as part of a mezze platter or as a standalone dish.

Turkish Imam Bayildi with Feta

Ingredients:

- 4 small to medium-sized eggplants
- 4 tablespoons olive oil, plus extra for drizzling
- 1 onion, finely chopped
- 3 cloves garlic, minced
- 2 tomatoes, diced
- 2 tablespoons tomato paste
- 1 teaspoon ground cumin
- 1 teaspoon paprika
- Salt and black pepper, to taste
- 1/4 cup chopped fresh parsley
- 1/4 cup crumbled Feta cheese
- Lemon wedges, for serving

Instructions:

Preheat the oven to 375°F (190°C).
Cut the eggplants in half lengthwise. Score the flesh with a knife in a criss-cross pattern, being careful not to cut through the skin.
Place the eggplant halves on a baking sheet lined with parchment paper. Drizzle with olive oil and season with salt and black pepper. Roast in the preheated oven for about 20-25 minutes, or until the flesh is tender.
While the eggplants are roasting, prepare the filling. In a large skillet, heat 2 tablespoons of olive oil over medium heat. Add the chopped onion and cook until softened, about 5 minutes. Add the minced garlic to the skillet and cook for another minute, until fragrant.
Stir in the diced tomatoes, tomato paste, ground cumin, and paprika. Cook for about 5 minutes, until the tomatoes start to break down and the mixture thickens slightly.
Season the filling with salt and black pepper, to taste. Stir in the chopped fresh parsley.
Remove the roasted eggplants from the oven and let them cool slightly. Once cooled, use a spoon to carefully scoop out some of the flesh from the eggplant halves, leaving a border around the edges.
Chop the scooped-out eggplant flesh and add it to the filling mixture in the skillet. Stir to combine.
Spoon the filling mixture into the hollowed-out eggplant halves, dividing it evenly among them.
Crumble Feta cheese over the top of each stuffed eggplant half.
Return the stuffed eggplants to the oven and bake for another 15-20 minutes, or until the Feta cheese is melted and golden brown.
Serve the Imam Bayildi with Feta hot or at room temperature, garnished with additional chopped parsley and lemon wedges on the side.

Enjoy your delicious Turkish Imam Bayildi with Feta cheese!

Moroccan Carrot Salad with Cumin Dressing

Ingredients:

For the salad:

- 4 large carrots, peeled and grated
- 1/4 cup chopped fresh cilantro or parsley
- 1/4 cup chopped toasted almonds or pistachios
- 2 tablespoons raisins or dried cranberries (optional)
- Salt and black pepper, to taste

For the cumin dressing:

- 2 tablespoons extra virgin olive oil
- 1 tablespoon lemon juice
- 1 teaspoon ground cumin
- 1/2 teaspoon ground coriander
- 1/2 teaspoon paprika
- 1/4 teaspoon ground cinnamon
- 1/4 teaspoon ground ginger
- Salt and black pepper, to taste

Instructions:

In a large mixing bowl, combine the grated carrots, chopped fresh cilantro or parsley, chopped toasted almonds or pistachios, and raisins or dried cranberries (if using). Toss to combine.
In a small bowl, whisk together the extra virgin olive oil, lemon juice, ground cumin, ground coriander, paprika, ground cinnamon, ground ginger, salt, and black pepper to make the cumin dressing.
Pour the cumin dressing over the carrot mixture in the large mixing bowl. Toss until the salad is evenly coated with the dressing.
Taste and adjust the seasoning, adding more salt, black pepper, or lemon juice if desired.
Cover the salad and refrigerate for at least 30 minutes to allow the flavors to meld together.
Serve the Moroccan Carrot Salad with Cumin Dressing chilled or at room temperature.
Garnish with additional chopped cilantro or parsley and toasted almonds or pistachios before serving, if desired.

Enjoy your delicious and vibrant Moroccan Carrot Salad with Cumin Dressing as a refreshing side dish or light meal!

Persian Adas Polo (Lentil Rice)

Ingredients:

- 1 cup basmati rice
- 1/2 cup brown lentils
- 1 onion, finely chopped
- 2 cloves garlic, minced
- 2 tablespoons olive oil
- 1/2 teaspoon ground turmeric
- 1/2 teaspoon ground cumin
- 1/2 teaspoon ground cinnamon
- Salt and black pepper, to taste
- 2 cups vegetable broth or water
- 1/4 cup chopped fresh parsley, for garnish
- 1/4 cup chopped toasted almonds or pistachios, for garnish (optional)

Instructions:

Rinse the basmati rice under cold water until the water runs clear. Drain well.
In a small bowl, cover the lentils with water and let them soak for about 30 minutes. Then, drain the lentils.
In a large skillet or pot, heat the olive oil over medium heat. Add the chopped onion and minced garlic, and sauté until softened and translucent, about 5 minutes.
Add the drained lentils to the skillet, along with ground turmeric, ground cumin, ground cinnamon, salt, and black pepper. Stir well to coat the lentils in the spices.
Add the basmati rice to the skillet and stir to combine with the lentils and spices.
Pour the vegetable broth or water over the rice and lentil mixture. Bring to a boil, then reduce the heat to low, cover, and simmer for about 15-20 minutes, or until the rice and lentils are cooked and tender and the liquid is absorbed.
Once the rice and lentils are cooked, remove the skillet from the heat and let it sit, covered, for about 5 minutes.
Fluff the Persian Adas Polo with a fork to separate the grains and distribute the lentils evenly throughout the rice.
Transfer the Adas Polo to a serving platter or dish. Garnish with chopped fresh parsley and toasted almonds or pistachios, if desired.
Serve the Persian Adas Polo hot as a delicious and nutritious main dish or side dish.

Enjoy your flavorful and aromatic Persian Adas Polo (Lentil Rice)!

Lebanese Mujadara with Mint Yogurt Sauce

Ingredients for Mujadara:

- 1 cup brown or green lentils
- 1 cup rice (long-grain or basmati)
- 3 large onions, thinly sliced
- 4 tablespoons olive oil
- 1 teaspoon cumin
- 1/2 teaspoon ground coriander
- Salt and pepper to taste
- Chopped parsley for garnish (optional)

Ingredients for Mint Yogurt Sauce:

- 1 cup plain yogurt
- 2 tablespoons chopped fresh mint leaves
- 1 clove garlic, minced
- 1 tablespoon lemon juice
- Salt to taste

Instructions:

Rinse the lentils under cold water and drain. In a medium saucepan, combine the lentils with 2 cups of water. Bring to a boil, then reduce heat and simmer for about 20-25 minutes, or until the lentils are tender but not mushy. Drain any excess water and set aside.
Rinse the rice under cold water until the water runs clear. In another saucepan, combine the rice with 2 cups of water. Bring to a boil, then reduce heat to low, cover, and simmer for about 15-20 minutes, or until the rice is cooked and fluffy. Remove from heat and let it sit, covered, for 5 minutes. Fluff the rice with a fork and set aside.
While the lentils and rice are cooking, heat 2 tablespoons of olive oil in a large skillet over medium heat. Add the sliced onions and cook, stirring frequently, until they are caramelized and golden brown, about 20-25 minutes. Remove half of the caramelized onions and set aside for garnish.
To the remaining onions in the skillet, add the cooked lentils, cooked rice, cumin, ground coriander, salt, and pepper. Stir to combine and cook for another 5-10 minutes, until heated through and well combined.
While the Mujadara is cooking, prepare the mint yogurt sauce. In a small bowl, mix together the plain yogurt, chopped mint leaves, minced garlic, lemon juice, and salt to taste. Stir until well combined.
Serve the Mujadara hot or warm, topped with the reserved caramelized onions and chopped parsley if desired. Serve the mint yogurt sauce on the side or drizzle it over the Mujadara before serving.

Enjoy your Lebanese Mujadara with Mint Yogurt Sauce as a satisfying and flavorful meal!

Feel free to adjust the seasoning and thickness of the yogurt sauce according to your taste preferences.

Turkish Stuffed Eggplant with Tomato Sauce

Ingredients:

For the stuffed eggplants:

- 4 medium-sized eggplants
- 2 tablespoons olive oil
- 1 onion, finely chopped
- 2 cloves garlic, minced
- 1/2 lb (225g) ground beef or lamb
- 2 tomatoes, diced
- 1 green bell pepper, diced
- 2 tablespoons tomato paste
- 1 teaspoon paprika
- 1/2 teaspoon ground cumin
- Salt and black pepper, to taste
- Fresh parsley, chopped, for garnish

For the tomato sauce:

- 2 tablespoons olive oil
- 2 tomatoes, diced
- 2 cloves garlic, minced
- 1 teaspoon paprika
- Salt and black pepper, to taste
- 1/2 cup water or vegetable broth

Instructions:

Preheat your oven to 375°F (190°C).
Wash the eggplants and cut them in half lengthwise. Score the flesh with a knife in a criss-cross pattern, being careful not to cut through the skin.
Place the eggplant halves on a baking sheet lined with parchment paper. Drizzle with olive oil and season with salt and black pepper. Roast in the preheated oven for about 20-25 minutes, or until the flesh is tender.
While the eggplants are roasting, prepare the stuffing. In a large skillet, heat 2 tablespoons of olive oil over medium heat. Add the chopped onion and minced garlic, and sauté until softened, about 5 minutes.
Add the ground beef or lamb to the skillet and cook until browned, breaking it up with a spoon as it cooks.

Stir in the diced tomatoes, diced green bell pepper, tomato paste, paprika, ground cumin, salt, and black pepper. Cook for another 5 minutes, until the vegetables are softened and the mixture is well combined. Remove from heat.

Once the eggplants are roasted, remove them from the oven and let them cool slightly. Use a spoon to carefully scoop out some of the flesh from the eggplant halves, leaving a border around the edges.

Chop the scooped-out eggplant flesh and add it to the stuffing mixture in the skillet. Stir to combine.

Stuff each eggplant half with the stuffing mixture, packing it in lightly.

In a separate saucepan, prepare the tomato sauce. Heat 2 tablespoons of olive oil over medium heat. Add the diced tomatoes and minced garlic, and cook for about 5 minutes, until the tomatoes start to break down.

Stir in the paprika, salt, black pepper, and water or vegetable broth. Bring the sauce to a simmer and cook for another 5 minutes.

Place the stuffed eggplants in a baking dish, cut side up. Pour the tomato sauce over the stuffed eggplants.

Cover the baking dish with aluminum foil and bake in the preheated oven for about 30-35 minutes, or until the eggplants are cooked through and the sauce is bubbly.

Remove the foil and bake for an additional 5-10 minutes, or until the sauce thickens slightly Garnish the Turkish Stuffed Eggplant with Tomato Sauce with chopped fresh parsley before serving.

Enjoy your delicious Turkish Stuffed Eggplant with Tomato Sauce as a flavorful and satisfying main dish!

Moroccan Zaalouk (Eggplant and Tomato Dip)

Ingredients:

- 2 large eggplants
- 2 tablespoons olive oil
- 4 cloves garlic, minced
- 2 tomatoes, diced
- 1 teaspoon paprika
- 1/2 teaspoon ground cumin
- 1/2 teaspoon ground coriander
- 1/4 teaspoon cayenne pepper (optional, for heat)
- Salt and black pepper, to taste
- Juice of 1 lemon
- Chopped fresh cilantro or parsley, for garnish

Instructions:

Preheat the oven to 400°F (200°C). Prick the eggplants all over with a fork and place them on a baking sheet lined with parchment paper. Roast in the preheated oven for about 40-45 minutes, or until the eggplants are very soft and collapsed.

Remove the eggplants from the oven and let them cool slightly. Once cool enough to handle, peel off and discard the skin.

In a large skillet or frying pan, heat the olive oil over medium heat. Add the minced garlic and cook for about 1 minute, until fragrant.

Add the diced tomatoes to the skillet and cook for about 5 minutes, until they begin to soften.

Mash the roasted eggplants with a fork or potato masher until smooth. Add the mashed eggplants to the skillet with the garlic and tomatoes.

Stir in the paprika, ground cumin, ground coriander, cayenne pepper (if using), salt, and black pepper. Cook for another 5-10 minutes, stirring occasionally, until the flavors are well combined and the mixture has thickened.

Remove the skillet from heat and stir in the lemon juice. Taste and adjust the seasoning, adding more salt, pepper, or lemon juice if needed.

Transfer the Zaalouk to a serving dish and garnish with chopped fresh cilantro or parsley. Serve the Moroccan Zaalouk warm or at room temperature as a dip or side dish. It can be enjoyed with crusty bread, pita, or as a topping for grilled meats or fish.

Enjoy your delicious and flavorful Moroccan Zaalouk!

Persian Kookoo Sabzi (Herb Frittata)

Ingredients:

- 2 cups chopped mixed fresh herbs (such as parsley, cilantro, dill, chives, and fenugreek)
- 6 large eggs
- 1 onion, finely chopped
- 2 cloves garlic, minced
- 1/2 cup walnuts, chopped (optional)
- 1/4 cup barberries (optional)
- 1/4 teaspoon ground turmeric
- 1/4 teaspoon ground cinnamon
- Salt and pepper to taste
- 2 tablespoons olive oil

Instructions:

Preheat your oven to 350°F (175°C).
In a large mixing bowl, beat the eggs until well combined.
Add the chopped herbs, onion, garlic, chopped walnuts (if using), barberries (if using), ground turmeric, ground cinnamon, salt, and pepper to the beaten eggs. Mix everything together until evenly combined.
Heat the olive oil in a large oven-safe skillet over medium heat.
Pour the egg and herb mixture into the skillet, spreading it out evenly.
Cook the kookoo sabzi for about 5-7 minutes on the stovetop, until the bottom is set and lightly golden brown.
Transfer the skillet to the preheated oven and bake for an additional 15-20 minutes, or until the kookoo sabzi is fully set and cooked through.
Once cooked, remove the skillet from the oven and let the kookoo sabzi cool for a few minutes.
Carefully slide the kookoo sabzi onto a serving platter or cutting board.
Slice the kookoo sabzi into wedges or squares and serve warm or at room temperature.
Enjoy your Persian Kookoo Sabzi as a delicious appetizer, side dish, or light meal!

Feel free to adjust the types and quantities of herbs according to your preference. You can also add other ingredients such as spinach or green onions for variation.

Lebanese Spinach Pies (Fatayer Sabanekh)

Ingredients:

For the dough:

- 3 cups all-purpose flour
- 1 teaspoon active dry yeast
- 1 teaspoon sugar
- 1 teaspoon salt
- 1 cup warm water
- 1/4 cup olive oil

For the spinach filling:

- 1 lb (450g) fresh spinach, washed and chopped
- 1 onion, finely chopped
- 2 cloves garlic, minced
- 2 tablespoons olive oil
- 1 tablespoon lemon juice
- 1 teaspoon ground sumac (optional)
- Salt and pepper, to taste

Instructions:

In a small bowl, dissolve the active dry yeast and sugar in warm water. Let it sit for about 5-10 minutes, until it becomes frothy.

In a large mixing bowl, combine the flour and salt. Make a well in the center and pour in the yeast mixture and olive oil. Mix until a dough forms.

Knead the dough on a floured surface for about 5-7 minutes, until it becomes smooth and elastic. Place the dough in a greased bowl, cover with a clean kitchen towel, and let it rise in a warm place for about 1 hour, or until doubled in size.

While the dough is rising, prepare the spinach filling. Heat 2 tablespoons of olive oil in a large skillet over medium heat. Add the chopped onion and minced garlic, and sauté until softened and translucent, about 5 minutes.

Add the chopped spinach to the skillet and cook until wilted, stirring occasionally, about 3-5 minutes.

Stir in the lemon juice and ground sumac (if using). Season with salt and pepper to taste.

Remove from heat and let the spinach mixture cool slightly.

Preheat your oven to 375°F (190°C). Line a baking sheet with parchment paper.

Once the dough has doubled in size, punch it down and divide it into 12 equal portions.

Roll out each portion of dough into a circle about 5-6 inches in diameter.

Place a spoonful of the spinach filling in the center of each dough circle.
Fold the edges of the dough over the filling, forming a triangle shape. Pinch the edges together to seal.
Place the spinach pies on the prepared baking sheet.
Bake in the preheated oven for about 15-20 minutes, or until the pies are golden brown.
Remove from the oven and let the spinach pies cool slightly before serving.
Enjoy your Lebanese Spinach Pies (Fatayer Sabanekh) warm or at room temperature as a delicious appetizer or snack!

Feel free to adjust the filling ingredients and spices according to your taste preferences. You can also add pine nuts or feta cheese to the spinach mixture for extra flavor.

Turkish Mezze Platter with Olives, Cheese, and Bread

Ingredients:

For the mezze platter:

- Assorted olives (such as green, black, and Kalamata olives)
- Turkish cheese varieties (such as beyaz peynir, kasar, or tulum cheese)
- Sliced cucumbers
- Sliced tomatoes
- Sliced bell peppers
- Sliced radishes
- Fresh herbs (such as parsley, mint, or dill)
- Turkish bread or pita bread, sliced or torn into pieces
- Optional: stuffed grape leaves (dolma), hummus, tzatziki, roasted red peppers, marinated artichoke hearts, roasted eggplant dip (baba ganoush), or any other favorite mezze dishes

Instructions:

Arrange the olives, cheese, sliced vegetables, and fresh herbs on a large platter or serving board. You can place them in small bowls or directly on the platter for a rustic presentation.

Add any optional mezze dishes you'd like to include, such as stuffed grape leaves, hummus, tzatziki, roasted red peppers, or roasted eggplant dip, to the platter.

Place the sliced or torn Turkish bread or pita bread on the platter alongside the other ingredients.

Garnish the mezze platter with additional fresh herbs for a pop of color and flavor.

Serve the Turkish mezze platter as a shared appetizer or snack, accompanied by your favorite beverages such as Turkish tea, ayran (yogurt drink), or wine.

Encourage guests to mix and match the different flavors and textures, and enjoy the variety of tastes that Turkish cuisine has to offer.

Enjoy your delicious Turkish mezze platter with olives, cheese, and bread with family and friends!

Feel free to customize the mezze platter with your favorite Turkish ingredients and dishes. The key is to offer a variety of flavors and textures for a delightful culinary experience.

Moroccan Lentil Salad with Roasted Vegetables

Ingredients:

For the lentil salad:

- 1 cup dried brown lentils, rinsed
- 3 cups water
- 1 red bell pepper, diced
- 1 yellow bell pepper, diced
- 1 zucchini, diced
- 1 small eggplant, diced
- 1 red onion, thinly sliced
- 3 tablespoons olive oil
- 2 teaspoons ground cumin
- 1 teaspoon ground coriander
- 1 teaspoon smoked paprika
- 1/2 teaspoon ground cinnamon
- Salt and black pepper, to taste
- Fresh cilantro or parsley, chopped, for garnish

For the dressing:

- 3 tablespoons extra virgin olive oil
- 2 tablespoons lemon juice
- 1 tablespoon honey or maple syrup
- 1 teaspoon ground cumin
- 1/2 teaspoon ground coriander
- 1/2 teaspoon smoked paprika
- Salt and black pepper, to taste

Instructions:

Preheat your oven to 400°F (200°C). Line a baking sheet with parchment paper.
In a large bowl, toss the diced bell peppers, zucchini, eggplant, and red onion with 3 tablespoons of olive oil, ground cumin, ground coriander, smoked paprika, ground cinnamon, salt, and black pepper until evenly coated.
Spread the seasoned vegetables in a single layer on the prepared baking sheet. Roast in the preheated oven for 25-30 minutes, or until the vegetables are tender and slightly caramelized, stirring halfway through the cooking time.
While the vegetables are roasting, prepare the lentils. In a medium saucepan, combine the rinsed lentils and water. Bring to a boil, then reduce heat to low, cover, and simmer for 20-25

minutes, or until the lentils are tender but not mushy. Drain any excess water and set aside to cool slightly.

In a small bowl, whisk together the extra virgin olive oil, lemon juice, honey or maple syrup, ground cumin, ground coriander, smoked paprika, salt, and black pepper to make the dressing.

In a large mixing bowl, combine the cooked lentils and roasted vegetables. Pour the dressing over the lentil and vegetable mixture and toss until evenly coated.

Taste and adjust the seasoning if needed, adding more salt, pepper, or lemon juice to taste.

Transfer the Moroccan Lentil Salad with Roasted Vegetables to a serving platter or bowl. Garnish with chopped fresh cilantro or parsley.

Serve the lentil salad warm, at room temperature, or chilled, depending on your preference. Enjoy your flavorful and nutritious Moroccan Lentil Salad with Roasted Vegetables as a satisfying main dish or side dish!

Feel free to customize this recipe by adding other roasted vegetables or spices according to your taste preferences. This salad can be enjoyed on its own, or served alongside grilled meats, fish, or crusty bread.

Persian Eggplant Stew (Gheimeh Bademjan)

Ingredients:

- 2 medium-sized eggplants
- 1 cup yellow split peas, rinsed
- 1 large onion, finely chopped
- 3 cloves garlic, minced
- 2 large tomatoes, diced
- 2 tablespoons tomato paste
- 1 teaspoon ground turmeric
- 1 teaspoon ground cinnamon
- 1/2 teaspoon ground cumin
- 1/4 teaspoon ground saffron (optional)
- Salt and black pepper, to taste
- 2 tablespoons vegetable oil or ghee
- 4 cups vegetable broth or water
- Juice of 1-2 lemons
- Fresh parsley or cilantro, chopped, for garnish

Instructions:

Peel the eggplants and cut them into thick slices. Place the eggplant slices in a colander and sprinkle with salt. Let them sit for about 20-30 minutes to release excess moisture and bitterness. Afterward, rinse the eggplant slices and pat them dry with paper towels.

In a large skillet or pot, heat the vegetable oil or ghee over medium heat. Add the chopped onion and minced garlic, and sauté until softened and golden brown, about 5-7 minutes.

Add the diced tomatoes, tomato paste, ground turmeric, ground cinnamon, ground cumin, ground saffron (if using), salt, and black pepper to the skillet. Cook for another 5 minutes, stirring occasionally, until the tomatoes begin to break down and the mixture becomes fragrant.

Add the rinsed yellow split peas to the skillet and stir to coat them in the tomato mixture. Pour in the vegetable broth or water and bring the mixture to a boil. Reduce the heat to low, cover, and simmer for about 20-25 minutes, or until the split peas are partially cooked.

Meanwhile, in a separate skillet or frying pan, heat a little oil over medium-high heat. Add the eggplant slices and fry them until golden brown on both sides, about 3-4 minutes per side. Remove the fried eggplant slices from the skillet and place them on a plate lined with paper towels to absorb any excess oil.

Once the split peas are partially cooked, add the fried eggplant slices to the skillet, arranging them on top of the stew. Cover and continue to simmer for another 20-25 minutes, or until the split peas are fully cooked and the eggplant is tender.

Taste the stew and adjust the seasoning if needed, adding more salt, pepper, or lemon juice to taste.

Just before serving, stir in the lemon juice to brighten the flavors of the stew.
Garnish the Persian Eggplant Stew (Gheimeh Bademjan) with chopped fresh parsley or cilantro.
Serve the stew hot, accompanied by steamed basmati rice or Iranian saffron rice, and enjoy the delicious flavors of this traditional Persian dish!

Feel free to adjust the seasoning and spice level of the stew according to your taste preferences.

You can also add diced potatoes or chunks of beef or lamb for additional flavor and protein.

Lebanese Lentil Salad with Feta and Mint

Ingredients:

For the salad:

- 1 cup dried green or brown lentils
- 2 cups water
- 1/2 cup crumbled feta cheese
- 1/4 cup chopped fresh mint leaves
- 1/4 cup chopped red onion
- 1/4 cup chopped cucumber
- 1/4 cup chopped cherry tomatoes
- 2 tablespoons extra virgin olive oil
- 2 tablespoons lemon juice
- Salt and black pepper, to taste

Instructions:

Rinse the lentils under cold water and drain. In a medium saucepan, combine the lentils and water. Bring to a boil, then reduce heat to low, cover, and simmer for about 20-25 minutes, or until the lentils are tender but not mushy. Drain any excess water and set aside to cool slightly.

In a large mixing bowl, combine the cooked lentils, crumbled feta cheese, chopped mint leaves, chopped red onion, chopped cucumber, and chopped cherry tomatoes.

In a small bowl, whisk together the extra virgin olive oil and lemon juice to make the dressing. Season with salt and black pepper to taste.

Pour the dressing over the lentil mixture in the large mixing bowl. Toss until all the ingredients are evenly coated with the dressing.

Taste and adjust the seasoning if needed, adding more salt, pepper, or lemon juice to taste.

Cover the lentil salad and refrigerate for at least 30 minutes to allow the flavors to meld together.

Before serving, give the lentil salad a quick stir. Garnish with additional chopped mint leaves if desired.

Serve the Lebanese Lentil Salad with Feta and Mint as a delicious and nutritious side dish or light meal.

Enjoy your flavorful and refreshing Lebanese Lentil Salad with Feta and Mint! It's perfect for picnics, potlucks, or as a healthy lunch option.

Turkish Börek with Potato and Cheese

Ingredients:

For the filling:

- 3 medium potatoes, peeled and thinly sliced
- 1 cup crumbled feta cheese (or any other cheese of your choice)
- 1/2 cup chopped parsley
- 1/2 cup chopped dill
- Salt and pepper to taste
- 2 tablespoons olive oil

For assembling the börek:

- 1 package of phyllo dough (about 12 sheets), thawed if frozen
- 1/2 cup melted butter or olive oil for brushing

Instructions:

Preheat your oven to 375°F (190°C). Grease a baking dish with olive oil or butter and set aside.

In a large mixing bowl, combine the thinly sliced potatoes, crumbled feta cheese, chopped parsley, chopped dill, salt, pepper, and olive oil. Toss until the ingredients are evenly distributed.

Lay out one sheet of phyllo dough on a clean work surface. Brush the entire surface with melted butter or olive oil.

Place another sheet of phyllo dough on top of the first one and brush with melted butter or olive oil. Repeat this process until you have used half of the phyllo sheets, stacking them on top of each other.

Spread half of the potato and cheese filling evenly over the stacked phyllo sheets.

Repeat the layering process with the remaining phyllo sheets, brushing each one with melted butter or olive oil and stacking them on top of each other.

Spread the remaining potato and cheese filling evenly over the top layer of phyllo sheets.

Carefully roll up the stacked phyllo sheets into a log shape. If using a rectangular baking dish, you can cut the log into smaller pieces to fit the dish.

Place the rolled börek in the prepared baking dish, seam side down.

Brush the top of the börek with any remaining melted butter or olive oil.

Bake in the preheated oven for 30-35 minutes, or until the börek is golden brown and crispy on top.

Remove from the oven and let the börek cool for a few minutes before slicing and serving

Serve the Turkish Börek with Potato and Cheese warm or at room temperature as a delicious appetizer or side dish.

Enjoy your flavorful and satisfying Turkish Börek with Potato and Cheese!

Moroccan Vegetable Bastilla

Ingredients:

For the vegetable filling:

- 2 tablespoons olive oil
- 1 onion, finely chopped
- 2 cloves garlic, minced
- 1 teaspoon ground cumin
- 1 teaspoon ground coriander
- 1/2 teaspoon ground cinnamon
- 1/4 teaspoon ground turmeric
- 1 cup diced carrots
- 1 cup diced zucchini
- 1 cup diced bell peppers (any color)
- 1 cup cooked chickpeas
- Salt and pepper to taste
- 1/4 cup chopped fresh parsley
- 1/4 cup chopped fresh cilantro
- 1/4 cup chopped dried apricots (optional)
- 1/4 cup chopped toasted almonds or pine nuts

For assembly:

- 10 sheets of phyllo dough, thawed if frozen
- 1/2 cup melted butter or olive oil
- 3 eggs, beaten
- 1/4 cup chopped fresh parsley and cilantro, for garnish
- Powdered sugar and ground cinnamon, for dusting (optional)

Instructions:

Preheat your oven to 375°F (190°C). Grease a 9-inch round baking dish or pie dish and set aside.
Heat the olive oil in a large skillet over medium heat. Add the chopped onion and minced garlic, and sauté until softened and translucent, about 5 minutes.
Add the ground cumin, ground coriander, ground cinnamon, and ground turmeric to the skillet. Stir to coat the onions and garlic in the spices.

Add the diced carrots, diced zucchini, and diced bell peppers to the skillet. Cook, stirring occasionally, until the vegetables are tender, about 8-10 minutes.

Stir in the cooked chickpeas, salt, pepper, chopped fresh parsley, chopped fresh cilantro, and chopped dried apricots (if using). Cook for another 2-3 minutes to combine the flavors.

Remove the skillet from the heat and stir in the chopped toasted almonds or pine nuts. Let the vegetable filling cool slightly.

Lay one sheet of phyllo dough on a clean work surface and brush it lightly with melted butter or olive oil. Place another sheet of phyllo dough on top and brush with melted butter or olive oil. Repeat this process until you have used half of the phyllo sheets, stacking them on top of each other.

Carefully transfer the stacked phyllo sheets to the prepared baking dish, allowing the edges to hang over the sides.

Spoon the cooled vegetable filling into the phyllo-lined baking dish and spread it out evenly.

Pour the beaten eggs over the vegetable filling, distributing them evenly.

Fold the overhanging phyllo dough over the top of the filling to encase it completely, creating a sealed packet.

Brush the top of the bastilla with any remaining melted butter or olive oil.

Bake in the preheated oven for 25-30 minutes, or until the phyllo dough is golden brown and crispy.

Remove from the oven and let the bastilla cool for a few minutes before slicing.

Garnish the Moroccan Vegetable Bastilla with chopped fresh parsley and cilantro.

Optional: Dust the top of the bastilla with powdered sugar and ground cinnamon for a sweet and savory flavor contrast.

Serve the bastilla warm as a delicious main dish or appetizer.

Enjoy your flavorful and aromatic Moroccan Vegetable Bastilla!

Persian Lentil and Spinach Soup (Ash-e Reshteh)

Ingredients:

- 1 cup green or brown lentils, rinsed and drained
- 1/2 cup chickpeas, soaked overnight (or canned, drained and rinsed)
- 1 large onion, chopped
- 3 cloves garlic, minced
- 1 bunch fresh spinach, washed and chopped
- 1 bunch fresh cilantro, chopped
- 1 bunch fresh parsley, chopped
- 1 bunch fresh dill, chopped
- 1/2 cup chopped green onions (scallions)
- 1/2 cup chopped chives
- 8 cups vegetable or chicken broth
- 1/2 cup vermicelli or linguine, broken into small pieces
- 1/2 teaspoon ground turmeric
- 1 teaspoon ground cumin
- 1/2 teaspoon ground cinnamon
- Salt and pepper to taste
- Olive oil for sautéing
- Greek yogurt (optional, for serving)
- Mint leaves (optional, for garnish)
- Lime or lemon wedges (optional, for serving)

Instructions:

Heat some olive oil in a large pot over medium heat. Add chopped onions and sauté until translucent, about 5 minutes. Add minced garlic and cook for another minute.

Stir in lentils and chickpeas, then add vegetable or chicken broth. Bring to a boil, then reduce heat to low and let it simmer for about 20 minutes, or until lentils and chickpeas are tender

Add chopped spinach, cilantro, parsley, dill, green onions, and chives to the pot. Stir well and let it simmer for another 10 minutes.

In a separate pan, heat some olive oil over medium heat. Add vermicelli or broken linguine and toast until golden brown, about 3-4 minutes.

Add toasted vermicelli to the soup pot. Stir in ground turmeric, ground cumin, ground cinnamon, salt, and pepper. Adjust seasoning according to your taste.

Let the soup simmer for an additional 10-15 minutes, allowing all the flavors to meld together.

Serve hot, garnished with a dollop of Greek yogurt, fresh mint leaves, and a squeeze of lime or lemon juice if desired.

Enjoy this nutritious and flavorful Persian Lentil and Spinach Soup with some warm bread on the side for a complete meal!